Played Out

THE RACE MAN IN TWENTY-FIRST-CENTURY SATIRE

BRANDON J. MANNING

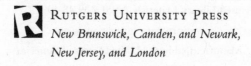
RUTGERS UNIVERSITY PRESS
New Brunswick, Camden, and Newark,
New Jersey, and London

LIBRARY OF CONGRESS CATALOGING-IN-PUBLICATION DATA

Names: Manning, Brandon J., 1984—author.
Title: Played out: the Race Man in twenty-first-century satire /
    Brandon J. Manning.
Description: New Brunswick: Rutgers University Press, [2022] |
    Includes bibliographical references and index.
Identifiers: LCCN 2021015637 | ISBN 9781978824249 (paperback) |
    ISBN 9781978824256 (hardback) | ISBN 9781978824263 (epub) |
    ISBN 9781978824270 (mobi) | ISBN 9781978824287 (pdf)
Subjects: LCSH: African Americans in the performing arts. | American
    fiction—African American authors—History and criticism. | Satire,
    American—History and criticism. | African Americans—Race
    identity. | African Americans—Intellectual life.
Classification: LCC PN1590.B53 M26 2022 | DDC 791.089/
    96073—dc23
LC record available at https://lccn.loc.gov/2021015637

A British Cataloging-in-Publication record for this book is available
from the British Library.

www.rutgersuniversitypress.org

Manufactured in the United States of America

*To my love, Johnnjalyn,
and our remarkable children:
Isaiah, Jaden, and Zuri*

Contents

Played Out

Introduction

Please Let Me Be Misunderstood—Black Masculine Vulnerabilities and the Ruse of Satire

In 2018, Kendrick Lamar opened the 60th Grammy Awards ceremony with a musical performance that he labeled a satire. The performance was a meditation on American racism, violence, and capitalism in the age of Trump. Lamar took his complex lyrics, jarring choreography, and vibrant images and offered a range of possibilities that lent on the Black satirical tradition. This appearance followed his 2016 Grammys performance of songs from his critically acclaimed album *To Pimp a Butterfly* (2015).[1] In both performances, Lamar leveraged the spectacle of Black rage against images of dispossession and despair. However, it is his incorporation of satire in his later performance that introspectively connected scenes of Black anger and resistance to America's insatiable desire to see Black men perform pain, despair, and anger. As such, Lamar's satire demonstrated an awareness of how American popular culture consumes and polices his racial and gender performance.

Lamar's 2018 performance begins with the song "XXX" from his Pulitzer Prize–winning fourth studio album *Damn* (2017).[2] A crooning voice sings "America, God Bless you if it's good to you." This highlights the precarity and proximity of Black subjectivity to the neoliberal state.[3] Men in army fatigues and ski masks march in place and change formation to reveal Lamar wearing a look of agony on his face under a spotlight.

1

Consoling a friend whose child is murdered, Lamar raps, "I know that you anointed, show me how to overcome / He was lookin' for some closure / Hopin' I could bring him closer / To the spiritual, my spirit do no better, but I told him / 'I can't sugar coat the answer for you / This is how I feel—if somebody kill my son / That mean somebody's gettin' killed.'" Lamar's lyrics demonstrate the tensions for him to perform the role of a modern-day race man in hip-hop; the historical formation of a singular leader for Black social, cultural, and political engagements around the central issue of race and racism. As a socially conscious rapper, people approach Lamar's music as an extension of his racial politics. As such, there's an assumption that he is available for spiritual and political guidance. Lamar's lyric "Hopin' I could bring him closer" is an intentionally vague description of the work of a contemporary race man. It is apt that the description is loose and that the listener does not know what Lamar would bring him closer to—be it spiritual, mental, or physical closure to start his ability to grieve. Lamar's lyrics illuminate the terror and anguish for Black men living through what Christina Sharpe writes as being in the wake—a space "to mourn and to illustrate the ways our individual lives are always swept up in the wake produced and determined, though not absolutely, by the afterlives of slavery."[4] Moreover, the song captures the stakes for Lamar being thrust into the role of leader amongst his friends. Although the lyrics and performance focus on the tormented friend, the viewer understands the toll that this kind of witnessing has on Lamar and the expectations for him to offer up any insights. Since Mamie Till, Black mothers have always been the face of the emotional toll of losing Black children to racialized violence and gun violence. However, the myth of the race man has often tasked Black leaders with trying to make sense out of senseless death. Lamar seemingly acknowledges this tradition of Black leadership as he distances himself from it by suggesting that he would respond to death with more

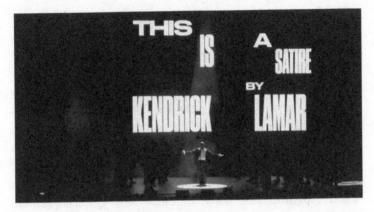

I.1. Kendrick Lamar labeling his performance a satire after performing his song "XXX" at the 2018 Grammy Awards ceremony.

death. The music ends abruptly, and the lights are turned off. A spotlight reveals Kendrick Lamar centerstage gesturing toward a screen behind him that reads "This is a satire by Kendrick Lamar" (Figure I.1).

By labeling his performance a satire, Kendrick Lamar evoked a tradition of Black men engaging in a public meaning-making process that foregrounds Black masculine emotionality and interiority while simultaneously inviting White consumption and misunderstanding. Black satire is a variant of the Black public intellectual tradition wherein White America renders Black masculinity hypervisible. The accolades that accompany such Black masculine performances celebrate them for their witticism and, most importantly, the ability to leave White audiences space to create their own meaning and laugh away what remains as either nonsensical or absurd. The Black satirical tradition presupposes that misrepresentation and misunderstanding are at the crux of understanding Black cultural production, and, in turn, satirists play on the obliviousness of White and Black America. The sonic space Lamar creates with his medley of songs provides a dialectic between overdetermined/stereotypical representations of blackness and Black interiority to demonstrate the difference between the ways Black people are thought of and situated in society versus their lived experiences.

The presence of famed satirist Dave Chappelle during the performance indexes the satirical tradition that Kendrick Lamar is entering into. Chappelle provides a brief interlude when he introduces himself and states, "The only thing more frightening than watching a black man be honest in America is being an honest black man in America." Chappelle's presence on stage reifies Lamar's performance as satirical: conveying the import of Lamar's performance while simultaneously gesturing toward Chappelle's own struggles with celebrity and creating satires that legibly critique white supremacy. As Chappelle describes the tradition of contemporary Black satirists functioning as truth-telling griots, his choice to foreground Black masculinity demonstrates the gendered ways Black men have become hyper-visible comedic subjects in the laughscape of American humor and satire.[5] Chappelle's commentary illuminates the subsequent stakes for Black men attempting to subvert American racial ideologies and humorous temperaments by evoking his decision to break a 50-million-dollar contract by leaving his hugely popular sketch comedy *Chappelle's Show* (2003–2006) during its third season. Chappelle situates himself as the audience member, his statement about watching alludes to how this moment conjures up negative feelings for him, and after he provides this aphorism about honest Black men the audience laughs presumably at both Lamar and Chappelle's past and present vulnerability. After another performance, the screen cuts back to Chappelle saying, "It looks like he is singing and dancing, but this brother is taking enormous chances. Rumble, Young Man, Rumble." When Chappelle references Lamar's singing and dancing he evokes the tradition of blackface minstrelsy that advanced racist, stereotypical performances of blackness for White audiences and White laughter. Chappelle suggests that Lamar's satire subverts

I.2. Kendrick Lamar performing his song "DNA" alongside masked dancers during the 2018 Grammy Awards ceremony.

the historical dialectic between racist laughter and Black performance, and his evocation of the late Muhammad Ali with "Rumble, Young Man, Rumble" illustrates the fight like quality Chappelle attaches to this dialectic (Figure I.2).

Played Out: The Race Man in Twenty-First-Century Satire privileges the novel and sketch comedy genres to examine how Black cultural producers in the twenty-first-century use satirical forms to undermine the myth of the race man by underscoring the significance of self-reflexivity and interiority in Black masculine performance and representation. As Charles A. Knight writes, "Genre may not disappear as an interpretive guide, but its force is weakened by the particular information that emerges from the text itself."[6] To that end, as much as *Played Out* draws upon the popularity of the novel and sketch comedy, it also grounds the critiques made within these pages and scenes to other genres like drama, film, music, visual art, and performances like Kendrick Lamar's at the Grammys in order to demonstrate the pervasiveness of these critiques. More broadly, this book draws upon and contributes to Black feminist theory, literary studies, performance studies, and humor studies by examining the veiled and subtle ways Black men invite audiences into their unique perspectives and emotional responses.

A SATIRICAL PEOPLE

Since the popularity of Bert Williams on the minstrel stage in the late nineteenth century and Uncle Julius in Charles Chesnutt's "conjure tales," America has had an insatiable desire for Black men to be persistent visual and literary sites of laughter.[7] Black male writers and cultural producers' initial response to stereotypical representation was to supplant these images with solemn heroic tales of blackness—specifically Black men that were worthy of equality and equal access to patriarchy. Even as Black men attempt to subvert the corrosiveness of blackface caricature, however, their bodies and lived experiences continue to be humorous fodder for America's consumptive laughter. I use "consumptive laughter" herein as a term to refer to the ways dominant culture often uses laughter to reduce, essentialize, and disregard Black experiences. Like Vincent Woodard, my use of "consumption" is rooted in "modern notions of market economies, commodities, consumer appetite" as a practice that illuminates in this contemporary moment the impact of neoliberal pressures of production for Black satirists.[8] The relationship between consumption and laughter is situated in laughter's inherent sociality. As sociologist Michael Billig asserts, "Humor is central to social life."[9] Consumptive laughter flattens Black rebellious humor and the ways in which the audience is implicated in issues of social critique and representation.

Despite dominant culture's desire to use humor as an oppressive tool for Black men and women, marginalized communities routinely use humor, and specifically satire, to subvert the political, social, and cultural realities of race and racism in America. For communities of color and queer communities, humor has long been a shared meaning-making process that accentuates precisely the juncture and disjuncture of our collective similarities. From the trickster figures of African folk traditions brought to the New World in the hulls of slavers and circulated on plantations in the eighteenth and nineteenth centuries to the comedy acts of the Chitlin' Circuit in the early to middle part of the twentieth century, and then later still to the sites of Black queer, camp, and funny disidentifications of the late twentieth century, levity has been one of the many ways in which marginalized people endure the traumas of the day by laughing into existence a hope and at times ambivalence about tomorrow.[10]

Living with and through the grotesque and absurd stereotypes and multivalent forms of racism, the condition of a thriving/ unbothered blackness is a satire on the American racial landscape, with the ironies of Black joy and resistance subverting a broader American grammar of exclusion, dispossession, and violence. Anytime Black people do not allow for racism and race to confine their reality, or they highlight the precarity of Black life in a country that projects an accessible American Dream, as Kendrick Lamar did in his 2018 Grammys performance, they subtly attack the white supremacist foundation of the nation-state. If we agree with Fred Moten that "the history of blackness is testament to the fact that objects can and do resist," then that resistance is a satire on the American racial landscape.[11]

According to Northrop Frye, satire requires two things: "One is wit or humor founded on fantasy or a sense of the grotesque or absurd, the other is an object of attack."[12] There is nothing more grotesque or absurd than the transatlantic slave trade and the intercontinental creation of race. Darryl Dickson-Carr outlines this process when he writes, "African Americans were forced to create various complex coded languages and expressions that allowed for the indirect expression of their frustration. Bitingly satiric humor was as much a part of these codes as any other rhetorical element, written into a language of indirection that often satisfied those who held power even as it stymied them."[13] The dehumanization of Black people in the hulls of slavers and their New World enslavement meant they required a precocious wit and humor to negotiate and undermine the peculiar institution of slavery. As Christina Sharpe asserts, "Slavery and the Middle Passage were ruptures with and a suspension of the known world that initiated enormous and ongoing psychic, temporal, and bodily breaches," but within the crevasses of these breaches formed various ways of being, resisting, and laughing.[14] Trickster figures, maroon colonies in the Caribbean, and a diasporic love of dancing to the brief downbeats of global anti-blackness are just some of the ways that Black people have historically claimed spaces for joy, humor, and play that defies the singularity of their marginalization.

BLACK SATIRICAL TRADITIONS

"Satire" is a troublesome word. Its meaning is as contested and ambiguous as some of the critiques leveled within satirical texts and performances. Historically, satire was thought of as for the well-traveled and intellectual and therefore was understood as predominantly White, masculine, and elitist. It has traditionally been divided into three categories: Menippean, Juvenalian, and Horatian. The different forms are stratified by the anger and scope of their object of attack. Juvenalian satire, named after the greatest Roman exponent of the form, Juvenal, is the most severe for its attack and derisiveness. Juvenalian satires attack governments, social norms, religion, and so on to dismantle their appropriative power. Menippean satire, named for the Greek philosopher Menippus, is a milder form that focuses on individual vices and folly or perspectives without the invective of Juvenalian satire. Conversely, Horatian satire, named for Roman poet Horace, is the lightest form of satire. Less invested in the attack and more invested in its humorous delivery, Horatian satire is more concerned with amusing the reader or viewer. Parody, irony, sarcasm, absurdity, and exaggeration are present throughout these forms.

Black men's satirical production comes at a cost. As noted satirical novelist and poet Paul Beatty once wrote, "Everything is satirical."[15] Beatty asserts satire's ubiquity while highlighting the dystopic lens through which he reads the world. A few years later in response to being asked if he considered himself a satirist, he said: "No, not at all. In my head it would limit what I could do, how I could write about something. I'm just writing. Some of it's funny. . . . I mean, I get it. But it's an easy way not to talk about anything else. . . . It's easy just to hide behind the humor, and then you don't have to talk about anything else."[16] Beatty's paradoxical position of reading everything as satire and yet not wanting to be a satirist captures Black writers' and Black cultural producers' complex relationship to creating art in an anti-Black world that not only misunderstands but intentionally obfuscates Black meaning-making processes. Furthermore, the proliferation of satire in this moment means that when people get caught saying racist, sexist, and homophobic statements they often label their comments as satire to lessen the impact of their statement, and "satire" often operates as a pithy tool to disseminate more overtly racist content.[17]

Black satire peels and scratches at the corners of blackness to question our most basic assumptions about race, gender, and class. The work of thinking through the complexities of blackness is a constant theme in Black cultural production across time and genre, but what makes satire a unique site of this work is its centering of folks already at the middle. As such, Black satirists center issues of race and racism as the primary objects of attack.[18] Black Americans have a rich history of creating humorous expressions and satirical narratives of their experiences in the United States. Satire draws from a rich oral tradition. Trickster figures like Br'er Rabbit, Anansi, and others use play and humor as a means to resist oppressive power structures.

As Dustin Griffin asserts, "Satire always emerges at particular times and places," and for Black cultural producers those times and places are on the tail end of major social, cultural, political advancement for Black America.[19] It was the shifting landscape of the Harlem Renaissance movement that inspired early novel-length satires. Alain Locke's collection *The New Negro* (1925) articulated the stakes and newness of the moment when he wrote, "Negro life is seizing upon its first chances for group expression and self-determination."[20] However, everyone did not agree with Locke and others' collective vision for Black life in the 1920s. George Schuyler's essay "The Negro-Art Hokum" (1926) attended to the ideological underpinnings of the New Negro movement by questioning if there was a cultural difference between Black Americans and White Americans.[21] Schuyler's essay and its emphasis on a singular American experience was the telos of his 1931 satirical novel *Black No More* where he imagines a world where Black people can be turned White.[22] Wallace Thurman's *Infants of the Spring* (1932) followed Schuyler's novel.[23] Both complicate the ideological underpinnings and cultural landscape of the Harlem Renaissance, and both center a host of characters as they re-create Harlem to think broadly about the assumptions and beliefs that the Harlem Renaissance required of Black and White people. As Dickson-Carr asserts, "During the New Negro's ascent and after his demise, satire allowed New Negroes, particularly the Niggeratti, to attack the vacuity they perceived in the heart of American institutions."[24]

Ralph Ellison's novel *Invisible Man* (1952) shifts the focus from critiquing the expanse of Black cultural movements to focusing on Black interiority and individualism—a stylistic move that defines contemporary Black satire's investment in Black subjectivity and interiority.[25] Ellison's novel created discourses about Black (in)visibility, education, and race men—all themes that are prevalent in contemporary Black satire. Although his text was firmly situated in a Jim Crow, mid-century moment, Ellison's use of interiority in the laughscape of Black satire reverberates in Black satirical production today, which shifts the paradigm from blackness's stunted subjectivity through the trope of invisibility to the hypervisibility of Black culture, blackness, and Black men.[26] Furthermore, while most literary scholars argue that parody, irony, and sarcasm can be standalone rhetorical tools, the nature of race and racism ensures that any use of these rhetorical tools is inherently satirical. What becomes parodic or ironic against the backdrop of American racial politics moves beyond simple mimesis and play into the arena of the subversive to produce larger commentary on the state of race and racism in America.

For instance, Mat Johnson's *Pym* (2011) is a satire that parodies an Edgar Allen Poe novel.[27] Johnson's novel is a parody of Poe's *The Narrative of Arthur Gordon Pym of Nantucket* (1838).[28] From the illustrations in the frontmatter of the novel to the plot and the focus on Poe's work, Johnson reimagines Poe's work for this contemporary moment. By centering race, *Pym* creates an exploration into the Africanist presence in Poe's work and, more broadly, the American literary canon. Ultimately, Johnson's novel illuminates Toni Morrison's claim in *Playing in the Dark* (1992) that "Africanism is the vehicle by which the American self knows itself as not enslaved, but free; not repulsive, but desirable; not helpless, but licensed and powerful."[29] Jaynes is a literary scholar in the field of African American literature who refuses to sit on his university's Diversity Committee. When he fails to get tenure, he tells the president that his work "is about finding the answer to why we have failed to truly become a postracial society. It's about finding the cure! A thousand Baldwin and Ellison essays can't do this, you have to go to the source, that's why I started focusing on Poe. If we can identify how the pathology of Whiteness was constructed, then we can learn how to dismantle it."[30] Johnson's protagonist suggests that Poe's novel is an exploration of blackness, which Johnson then replicates and parodies as a contemporary exploration of whiteness, as he replicates Poe's pitfalls in his novel. On the surface, *Pym* as a parody directly engages and evokes Poe's novel. However, when we consider the larger ramifications of Johnson attending to Poe's fictive whitewashing of an actual account of the novel evoking the historical and literary violence then we recognize the political ramifications for Black people reclaiming their stories. Johnson's investment in reclaiming Black stories evokes a similar tradition as Ishmael Reed's *Flight to Canada* (1976) where Reed criticizes Harriet Beecher Stowe for stealing Josiah Henson's story.[31] In *Flight to Canada*, Reed criticizes Harriet Beecher Stowe's *Uncle Tom's Cabin* (1852) and its theft of Josiah Henson's *The Life of Josiah Henson, Formerly a Slave, Now an Inhabitant of Canada, as Narrated by Himself* (1849).[32] When a Black cultural producer parodies a White cultural producer's work, it is an attack on the state of whiteness and our contemporary and historical articulations of race; the exaggeration of form and content lays bare the impossibility of Black subjects inhabiting the space.

In African American literature, satire follows major artistic moments—principally the Harlem Renaissance and Black Arts movement—as sites of critique on issues of race, gender, class, and sexuality. There is a repeated cycle that can be detected in the production of Black satire over the last hundred years. First, Black politicians, leaders, and artists periodically responded to social, political, and cultural movements and events and, after each of these moments, satirists responded to their representations of Black life and leadership. While I have already discussed the Harlem Renaissance through the lens of Schuyler and Hughes, the political, social, and cultural stakes shifted for the Black Arts Movement.

Novels like Sam Greenlee's *The Spoke Who Sat by the Door* (1969), John Oliver Killens's *The Cotillion, or, One Good Bull Is Half the Herd* (1971), Ishmael Reed's *Mumbo Jumbo* (1972), and Fran Ross's *Oreo* (1974) all used humor and wit to attend to formations of race of racism during the Black Power and Black Arts movements.[33] Alongside these literary satires, the rise of Richard Pryor's stand-up comedy and, more specifically, his short-lived sketch comedy show *The Richard Pryor Show* (1977), helped to create a televisual space for Black satire during the 1970s.[34] Similarly, visual artists like Robert Colescott—who painted *George Washington Carver Crossing the Delaware: Page from an American History Textbook* (1975)—helped to incorporate satire into the growing body of critique around the U.S. bicentennial in 1976.

With the growth of Black cinema, popular culture, and multiculturalism, Black satire had its third wave in the 1990s and early 2000s. Satirical novels like Trey Ellis's *Platitudes* (1988), Darius James's *Negrophobia* (1992), Paul Beatty's *The White Boy Shuffle* (1996), and the spoofs of the Wayans Brothers, such as those seen in the film *Don't Be a Menace in South Central while Drinking Your Juice in the Hood* (1996) and the sketch comedy television show *In Living Color* (1990–1994), all helped to chart the shifting landscape of Black representation and performance in the late twentieth century.[35] Contributing to the performative representation of Black satire, Robert Townsend's film *Hollywood Shuffle* (1987), George C. Wolfe's play *The Colored Museum* (1987), Chris Rock's film *CB4* (1993), as well as *The Chris Rock Show* (1997–2000), all subverted images of blackness in popular culture.[36] The early 2000s spawned novels like Percival Everett's *Erasure* (2001) and films like Spike Lee's *Bamboozled* (2000) that continued the tradition of Black satirists attending to rigid definitions of blackness in their work.[37]

In the twenty-first century, artists are using new media and the internet to level their social commentary. damali ayo, for example, published the manual *How to Rent a Negro* (2005) and created a satirical website where White people can "rent" a Black person to help with their cultural currency at work, school, and home.[38] *Played Out* begins at this early twenty-first-century moment to think through issues of Black masculine authenticity and authority in satirical novels and sketch comedy shows like Paul Beatty's *The Sellout* and Dave Chappelle's *Show*.

I put these different genres and artistic platforms in conversation with one another to show how satirists across art forms focus on disrupting our notions of blackness.

BLACK MEN, SATIRE, AND THE ATTACKS ON BLACK FEMINISM

Throughout this genealogy of satire, the telos of Black critique is the subversion of our assumptions about blackness; however, these critiques of race are also inextricably tied to various gender performances for both Black men and women. Between the satirical production of the Black Arts movement and the 1990s, Black women writers and Black feminists began to articulate the intersectional site of Black women's oppression and erasure. Significantly, in the late 1980s Black men used satire as a space to voice their criticism of the popularity of Black women writers and the representation of Black men in their work. Black men's responses to Alice Walker's *The Color Purple* (1982) are a defining feature of a number of satirical works in this moment.[39]

Ishmael Reed, one of the more notable satirists of the late twentieth century, created a progeny of Black male satirists that continue to struggle to support Black women writers in their work. For instance, Reed refers to the depiction of Black men in *The Color Purple* and the film adaptation as a "Nazi conspiracy." In his novel *Reckless Eyeballing* (1986), Reed extends his anger toward Alice Walker through his fictional character Tremonisha Smarts, a successful Black feminist playwright.[40] Smarts gains critical acclaim for her play *Wrongheaded Man*, a drama about a Black man who abuses and rapes women throughout the play. Reed's novel sadistically attends to success of Walker's work through his character Flower Phantom, a man that shaves Black feminists' hair throughout the novel: "A man . . . tied her up, and shaved all of her hair off. His twisted explanation: this is what the French Resistance did to those women who collaborated with the Nazis. The man had said that because of her 'blood libel' of Black men, she was doing the same thing. Collaborating with the enemies of black men."[41] Ultimately, the novel ends with Tremonisha and another successful Black feminist playwright recognizing the error in their ways and promising to not create any more negative depictions of Black men. Reed's novel serves as a satirical landscape where he can first punish and then forgive Black feminists that critique Black men. Similarly, in Trey Ellis's *Platitudes* (1988), the writer protagonist Dewayne Wellington struggles to convince Isshee Ayam, a thinly veiled representation of Alice Walker, about the importance of representing Black boyhood as a modern, urban, girl-crazed, awkward form of blackness.[42] The novel is about writers and writing, and centers an interpolated novel in epistolary form—an overt reference to Walker's *The Color Purple*.[43] By the novel's end, Dewayne finishes his book and is sexually aroused at the thought of creating his narrative of Black boyhood without succumbing to the aesthetic choices of Isshee, and the novel ends with him going to have sex with Isshee arguably as sexual manifestation of his intellectual conquest. The sexist logic that undergirds Trey Ellis's novel is present in his title. For Ellis, the "platitudes" are Black women's static representation of Black men and Black life, and Ellis's novel argues that Black men need to regain control of their image. The vestiges of Black men using satire to critique Black feminism are also present in Percival Everett's *Erasure*. Everett's Black male writer protagonist struggles with the publishing industry and what he sees as a limited and stereotypical understanding of Blackness. Everett's protagonist is frustrated by the market success of Juanita Mae Jenkins, a fictitious Black woman writer who evokes the success and themes of Sapphire's *Push* (1996).[44] While Everett does not directly engage Alice Walker's work, it is important to note that Sapphire has stated that *Push* "was born out of *The Color Purple*."[45] Sapphire situates herself in the matrilineal line of Zora Neale Hurston, Toni Morrison, and most importantly, Alice Walker. Although Everett's protagonist does not engage in the same overt sexist actions of shaving Black women's heads or needing to sexually conquer them, his critique of her work and the way it gets essentialized as the Black experience reproduces a slightly less problematic version of this line of critique dating back to Reed.

Of these satires, George C. Wolfe's play *The Colored Museum* arguably best exemplifies how Black men have used satire to critique Walker's *The Color Purple*.[46] The drama is a series of satirical vignettes of Black life, and in the section "Symbiosis" Wolfe represents how Black men have to relinquish some of their blackness *and* manliness in order to advance in a 1980s America. An unnamed Black man takes his briefcase to a dumpster and begins to throw away his prized childhood possessions—music, literature, autographs that are all indicative of the radical Black popular culture of the 1960s and 1970s. A young Black kid enters the stage as the personification of the Black man's childhood and begins to ask why he is throwing away objects that are at the center of his identity. The man starts throwing away a second round of objects, including Eldridge Cleaver's *Souls on Ice* (1968).[47] When the Kid asks him what he is replacing it with, the man says *The Color Purple*. Horrified, the kid responds, "No!"[48] Cleaver's memoir, *Souls on Ice* is the linchpin of an angry Black masculine liberationist tradition founded on patriarchy and homophobia in its attempt to articulate a radical path toward freedom. Cleaver's anger toward Black gay men and women in *Souls* unmistakably marks his vision for Black liberation as a singular vision for heteronormative Black men. As such, Cleaver uses the fear of figurative castration as a tactic to argue for more hypermasculinity. It is precisely this metaphor and intellectual tradition of "fear of castration" that *The Colored Museum*'s kid evokes in his "No!" Whereas all of the objects prior to the mention of Cleaver's and Walker's works foreground a genderless representation of blackness, the inclusion of *Souls on Ice* and its replacement, *The Color Purple*, suggests the pressure the character feels to change his gender performance from a site of hypermasculinity to a more inclusive introspective performance of Black masculinity.[49]

I offer up these short examples of Black men using misogynoir in their satire to show how humor and satire are often weaponized against Black women.[50] Moya Bailey and Trudy coined "misogynoir" as a way to attend to and name the ways "that straight Black men were always instructing Black women about what to do with their bodies. So much of what was presented as the ways Black men and women relate to each other was an assumed heterosexual cis desire about how Black women were failing at being desirable."[51] For Black satire, misogynoir highlights the ways that cis-gendered, heterosexual Black male satirists tell Black women what and how their art and cultural production should attend to. Ultimately, it is through the lens of this type of misogynoir in satire that Black men express their frustration over the commercial success and desirability for Black women's work. As Black men argue for a more nuance understanding of identity and self-expression against the backdrop of American racial politics, they often do so at the expense of Black women in their work. Black male satirists center Black male protagonists and in doing so create more expansive articulations of Black masculinities in their satirical work. The humorous sensibilities of these visual and literary texts usually align with those of the Black male protagonists, and so it is their worldview that the audience understands and empathizes with. Black women are not afforded the same level of complexity and nuance, which means that any joke, any fleeting moment of introspection, has larger reverberations and outcomes oftentimes at the expense of Black women's subjectivity within these satirical laughscapes.

Moreover, it is Black men that primarily write, produce, and act in the social commentaries of Black satire. The overrepresentation of Black men means that it is their experiences, voices, and sensibilities that offer up some of our most salient forms of social critique on race. As stated above, the popularity of men in this genre is a direct result of the ways that Black men are situated as perennial funny men in America dating back to blackface minstrelsy, and a broader sign of American patriarchy's hatred of funny Black women. Within the larger American laughscape, men continuously question the ability of women comediennes and satirists to be funny in the twenty-first century. Christopher Hitchens, for example, infamously wrote an article in *Vanity Fair* titled "Why Women Aren't Funny."[52] Similarly, Kenan Thompson blamed Black women for not being funny enough for the lack of Black women's representation on *Saturday Night Live* (*SNL*), the longest-running sketch comedy TV show.[53] However, scholars like Linda Mizejewski have demonstrated how vital women's comedy is and how it "has become a primary site in mainstream pop culture where feminism speaks, talks back, and is contested."[54]

Historically, satire has been reserved for well-traveled men, meaning their biting critiques and social commentaries can easily be critiqued as thinly veiled performances of misogyny and elitism. Charles Knight writes about this gender disparity in satire when he suggests that historically it has been satire's investment in public discourse as a transgressive form that has largely made it a masculine pursuit.[55] For contemporary African American literature and cultural production, these historical interpretations of the preponderance of men in satire are not as relevant. Black women cultural producers have a long and robust history of using their work to engage in public discourse and of transgressing genre norms to do so. However, as Darryl Dickson-Carr states, "Satire has tended to be associated most closely with male writers and is therefore dominated by men."[56]

The continued lack of visibility of Black women within satire is in part because of the patriarchal landscape of the funny man. Satire offers the satirist a creative way of using indirection and distance as a mode of critique. Black women cultural producers routinely use concepts like community and kinship in ways that undermine this investment in distance, while Black men's cultural production has readily taken up this perspective as a generative space to speak from. The satirist has to accept a willingness for their audience to misunderstand their work, and this misunderstanding cultivates the audience and various levels of critique that the satirist is invested in making. This difference speaks to the way that American patriarchy has been interested in the project of American Black masculinity. By exploiting Black men's desires for racial equality, American patriarchy has offered literary, cinematic, and other modes of cultural production to Black men, allowing them to offer up a perspective of the Black experience that situates Black men as the ultimate signifier for blackness. Instead of naming both white supremacy and heteropatriarchy as overlapping oppressive forces that seek to confine Black men's gender and racial performances, Black men often use the discourse of crisis to enumerate their lack of parity along racial and gender lines with their White male counterparts. As Simone Drake reminds us in *When We Imagine Grace*, when Black masculinity is only connected to the specter of crisis it erases histories of Black men's self-determination and attempts to erase the ways that Black women and girls are more vulnerable to these overlapping oppressive structures.[57] *Played Out* interrogates the hypervisibility of Black men in satire in order to deconstruct what this heightened visibility produces for Black masculine cultural producers.

When I tell people I work at the intersection of Black masculinity and satire, the primary response I get in Black communities—specifically Black men—is the assumption that my work addresses the *problem* of Black men dressing in drag in comedic spaces. That primary assumption reiterates the troubling dialectic that Black satirists created around their critiques of Black feminism. More specifically, that misplaced investment in my

work embodies the argument that Wolfe makes in "Symbiosis"—
that Black men have to emasculate themselves within corporate
America and popular culture in order to advance their careers.
The fear of emasculation is clearly linked to a fear of gay
Black men and the boundaries around blackness that Black
nationalism advances. This line of critique centers patriarchal discourses that suggest that any blurring of gender lines or alignment
with Black women compromises Black men's power and ability
to respond to and resist white supremacist structures. Indeed,
these representations are often problematic not for their "effeminate" representation of Black masculinity but for their stereotypical representation of Black women. Such representations often
function as no more than blackface caricature of Black women,
especially Black matriarchs, as a way to undermine their power
and place within Black family structures. Characters like Tyler
Perry's Madea and Martin Lawrence's Big Momma and Sheneneh
have created a tradition of Black men performing in drag, and it
was Kenan Thompson's refusal to dress in drag—as part of this
cultural logic—that prompted his statement above about Black
women not being ready for SNL. Although Played Out centers
Black men's humorous and satiric expressions, it does not center
these masculinist critiques.[58]

Played Out examines how the production of various modes
of vulnerability in contemporary satire critique stereotypical
representations of both blackness and masculinity in the African
American literary and cultural imaginaries. The book argues that
contemporary satire is a site of Black masculine self-expression
and that Black male satirists use their vulnerability to trouble
discourses on race and gender in the post–civil rights era. I assert
that satire affords Black cultural producers the possibility to create vulnerable subjectivities that provide alternative models for
Black masculinity in the twenty-first century. I define this vulnerability as (1) an invitation for readers and viewers to laugh at
the Black male speaker-narrator—an act that disrupts Black

masculine performances of coolness, confidence, and physicality; (2) the creation of a Black masculine interiority and emotionality that has the potential to undermine the formation of misogyny by decentering Black men in contemporary sociopolitical spaces; and (3) a performance of ambivalence toward being misunderstood. Black masculine vulnerability is not a panacea for problems plaguing Black men, women, and communities, but I argue its representation is a necessary starting place to intervene in rejecting white supremacist heteropatriarchal structures and begin the process of decentering Black men from our social, cultural, and political structures.

Throughout *Played Out*, I use vulnerability as an organizing ideal that annunciates self-love, resistance, and collaboration. I arrived at vulnerability from various intellectual traditions, the first of which is contemporary feminist scholarship—notably the work of Judith Butler and her writing on vulnerability and resistance. According to Butler, Zeynep Gambetti, and Leticia Sabsay, "The point is to show that vulnerability is part of resistance, made manifest by new forms of embodied political interventions and modes of alliance that are characterized by interdependency and public action."[59] Within this theoretical framework, vulnerability is a response to precarity and therefore functions as the motivating force to engender change to oppressive biopolitical structures. Throughout their book, Butler, Gambetti, and Sabsay demonstrate the ways in which our interdependence resists paternalist structures of power—that is, the privatization of neoliberalism—and that it therefore has a built-in critique of masculinist and patriarchal configurations. They center corporeality and material conditions to think about people's need for one another, especially the dispossessed and disenfranchised—the makings of coalition building, solidarity, and the commons. I depart from their general use of vulnerability herein to center the psychosocial potential of vulnerability for Black men to subvert patriarchal formations.

My focus on Black masculine vulnerability is also indebted to the multifaceted ways that Black feminism annunciates Black men's relationship to patriarchy—and the emotional and psychological stakes of that relationship. More specifically, Black feminist scholarship's investment in troubling the relationship between Black men and American patriarchy informs much of my framework and construction of Black masculine vulnerability. When scholars like Hortense Spillers and others call for Black men to reject a broader American patriarchy, they in part mean for Black men to be vulnerable subjects by being emotionally and psychologically accessible. For instance, in "Mama's Baby, Papa's Maybe" Spillers writes, "It is the heritage off the mother that the African-American male must regain as an aspect of his own personhood—the power off 'yes' to the 'female' within."[60] If we, as Spillers suggests, strip away the "layers of attenuated meaning," the mother represents an ethnocentric Afro-diasporic representation of communal vulnerability that she argues men have lost because of their embrace of American patriarchy.

Sherley Anne Williams's critique of Black masculine heroic tales is an organizing ideal for *Played Out*. In "Some Implications of a Womanist Theory," Williams writes, "Having confronted what black men have said about [black women], it is now time for black feminist critics to confront—and to confront black male writers—with what they have said about themselves."[61] Williams seminal text goes on to outline the ways in which Black men have situated themselves as the heroes in their own stories, and links that heroism to an underlying patriarchal thought process. Williams's provocative call to confront Black male writers with what they have said about themselves is also a call to think beyond the Black masculine hero. As demonstrated above, Black men's satirical production is hypervisible and therefore functions as a ripe site for Williams's analysis, and Black male satirists routinely create Black male protagonists that are antiheroes. The move from hero to antihero is an important shift, and *Played Out* is a meditation on what this shift means for Black masculine representation. How do antiheroes respond to hypermasculinity? Are narratives of anti-heroes inherently nonpatriarchal?

Played Out argues that the use of vulnerability in con-temporary Black satire centers Black masculine interiority and foregrounds emotions to subvert dominant representations of Black hypermasculinity. The discourse of vulnerability in Afri-can American literature and culture has largely been constituted around Black subjects' relationship to state violence and Black women's multiple sites of oppression. Adding to the archive, Black queer theory's examination of abjection and abasement generates a broader field of inquiry into the potential of vulner-ability. *Played Out* rethinks the potential of vulnerability as it pertains to Black masculine subjects by arguing that the high stakes for Black men producing humor creates an intentional site of catharsis, community building, and an embrace of being misunderstood. Black men's ability to center their emotional and inner lives is foregrounded throughout the book.

The Black funny man has become a legible fixture of Black masculine performance. The overdetermined representation of Black masculinities in dominant culture foregrounds the body as it collectively claims authenticity over large swaths of Black men. Consequently, the subversive work of vulnerability centers the interiority of individual Black men and calls into question any claims of authenticity to argue for the legitimacy of various nuanced and capacious sites of Black masculinities. *Played Out* argues for a reading and viewing practice that looks beyond these stereotypical sites of Black masculinity to embrace how Black men present themselves vulnerably in a society that desires "hard" Black men—men that can endure racism; men that can take a joke and be laughed at rather than laughed with. Reflect-ing the interdisciplinary nature of my project, I analyze both lit-erary and visual satirical representations to underscore the broad cultural shifts in the reimagining of Black masculinity in the twenty-first century as Black men desire more control over their image and message. As such, I employ the analytical and methodological tools of Black feminist and Black queer theories, specifically the growing body of scholarship of Black affect studies, as well as literary studies and performance studies to examine Paul Beatty's novel *The Sellout* (2016), Dave Chappelle's satirical sketch comedy *Chappelle's Show* (2003–2006), Percival Everett's novel *I Am Not Sidney Poitier* (2009), and Keegan-Michael Key and Jordan Peele's sketch comedy show *Key and Peele* (2012–2015).[62] *Played Out* frames the potential of vulnerability in these popular texts as both engendering change within the narrative and representational sites of Black masculinity and illuminating the unavoidable pitfalls of marrying messages of vulnerability to humor.

Played Out takes up satires in the years leading up to and throughout the Obama era. These cultural texts think through representations and performances of Black masculinity in the twenty-first century and the relationship between vulnerability, masculinity, and neoliberalism during America's first Black presidency and the post–civil rights moment Obama exemplified. The Obama presidency accentuated civil rights discourse and narratives about the power of integration and helped to create a national narrative of racial progress that reimagined and romanticized a national politic that embraced the civil rights movement. The organizing structure tethered to Obama's presidency maintained a persistent representation of Black masculinity for the nation-state, and at the intersection of his criticized public performances of the presidency, of blackness, and of masculinity was an inexhaustible site for the policing of Black masculine emotionality.

THE NEO-LIBERAL RACE MAN?

I use "neoliberalism" throughout *Played Out* to mean the proliferation of private and corporate interests in public life and the use of corporate logic in noncorporate spaces in the late twentieth century to the present. Ultimately, the increase in privatization as a logic of late capital justifies labor production and maximizes labor, materialism, and consumerism. Neoliberalism's ability to maximize labor and consumerism acts as an organizing ethos of our social, political, and cultural spaces. Neoliberalism puts unique pressures on Black communities as a way of undermining investments in public spaces that were once invested in communal rather than private interests. This move of late capitalism comes at a moment where historic Black communities are now gentrified and fractured, so that physical spaces that were once predominantly Black and public are now increasingly White and privatized.

Neoliberalism enhances already problematic articulations of respectable Black masculinity in the twenty-first century. Here, I mean "respectable" to encompass cis-gendered, heteronormative Black men that operate along middle-class values and embody historical expressions of racial uplift. As Roderick Ferguson asserts in *The Reorder of Things*, since its inception with the Combahee River Collective in the 1970s, Black feminism has always antagonized neoliberal structures with the way that it calls out the white supremacist heteropatriarchy for anchoring neoliberal sentiment.[63] The confluence of white supremacist, heteropatriarchy and neoliberalism act as a less hostile socioeconomic regime that contours to the nuance of the post–civil rights moment. Stated differently, through its investment in marketability and materialism neoliberalism often makes the disenfranchisement and dispossession of poor people and people of color a common-sense outcome to contemporary socioeconomic needs. Respectable Black masculinity, or modern interpretations of the race man, then partially buy into some of these oppressive structures. Black men routinely gravitate toward the trope of the race man for the way it privileges men and creates homosocial order that, in the early twenty-first century, helps to render various initiatives and communities legible by re-creating civil rights–era discourse and representation.

For the would-be race man, self-branding and side hustles are sites of neoliberal enterprise. Branding becomes one of the primary ways that Black men seek to perform the race man motif, primarily through dress and a well-curated social media presence. Having its origins in more urban epicenters, hustling on the other hand takes on a more dynamic understanding than its origin. In *Decoded* (2010), Jay Z writes, "Hustling is the ultimate metaphor for the basic human struggles: the struggle to survive and resist, the struggle to win and to make sense of it all."[64] Beyond Jay Z's treatment of hustling as a metaphor, hustling is largely synonymous with selling illegal drugs. This definition can encompass other forms of illegal transactions. Although Jay Z cites the street corner and his selling of drugs as the underpinnings of his articulation of hustling above, it is his business acumen later in life that better aligns with how hustling enters into the dialectic space of the race man in the twenty-first century. Through the discourse of "hustling" and "grinding," respectable Black men that buy into the fiction of the race man monetize the desire for messianic Black male leadership as a privatized good. They create economies around education, mentorship, sports, and a cadre of other sites that were once communal and public in nature and refocus these spaces to create revenue and brand recognition. What is also embedded in these terms is the dogged approach to creating capital—both "grinding" and "hustling" imply an incessant commitment to creating and maintaining revenue-generating spaces.

It is important to stress that *Played Out* focuses on cis-gendered heteronormative representations of Black masculinity, which is to say that this project examines heterosexual, would-be respectable performances of Black masculinity. As such, this book thinks through how cis-het Black men attempt to wrestle with ideas around Black masculinity and how they can begin to decenter themselves from the social, cultural, and political landscape of

Black communities. Black satire laughs at our most basic assumptions about race, class, and gender. Why then focus on Black masculinities within contemporary Black satire? Black men in the pages and on the screens of Black satirical productions function as canaries in the coal mine of Black heteropatriarchy. Black satirists represent Black male characters firmly inside heteronormative identity categories and imbue them with conflicting points of view that challenge the power and desirability of dominant ideologies. The insider/outsider paradigm creates a dialectic between the alterity of the characters and dominant narratives of race and gender. This dialectic creates a tension between what is expected of Black boy and men characters negotiating issues of race. Through the use of subversion, irony, parody, and exaggeration, these characters' unique responses to American racial politics offer up alternate modes of blackness, masculinity, and race work. Instead of attacking dominant ideologies from the margins, these would-be patriarchs and race men create foils of Black masculinist ideology.

Black men representing Black men in the pages of novels and sketches are at the margin of normativity and nonnormativity. They are liminal subjects that disidentify with dominant discourses of race and gender through their performances of blackness and masculinity. As E. Patrick Johnson notes in *Appropriating Blackness*, there is power and security in mapping the margins of blackness, but satirists intentionally eschew this by distorting these boundaries.[65] Satirists call into question social, cultural, and political boundaries and their relationship to blackness while subtly creating a psychic space of recusal. Although popular Black satire rarely centers queer subjectivities and issues, it performs and embodies a broader queerness in its gender and racial performances through the recognition and subsequent avoidance of constitutive *proper* performances of Black masculinity.

The first chapter examines the underlying gender politics of hope and Black nihilism and how they create a theoretical paradigm for Black men to engage and disengage from the fictions of the race man. I engage these bodies of scholarship through the close readings of W.E.B. Du Bois's twentieth-century sense of "striving" and Paul Beatty's twenty-first-century embrace of Black nihilism in *The Sellout*. For Du Bois in *The Souls of Black Folk* (1903), striving produces an integrationist idyllic state where Black citizenry and, more specifically, Black manhood are actualized through a deep psychological, spiritual, and intellectual effort— an irrepressible reservoir of hope personified in the trope of the race man.[66] Whereas Du Bois articulates striving as a psychology for Black people to combat the hardships of Jim Crow, Beatty's use of Black nihilism in *Sellout* argues for a kind of psychological stillness for Black people in a post–civil rights America. This stillness reads for some in the novel as a site of intentional failure for the way it refuses to perform or articulate a proper blackness, but I argue it highlights how Black men embracing ambivalence and nothingness can disrupt our collective investment in the race man trope.

The second chapter explores Dave Chappelle's abrupt departure from *Chappelle's Show* by foregrounding his vulnerability in forcing America to "tour through a young black man's subconscious." Chappelle's meditation on laughter and vulnerability is dramatized in the performance and reception of his final sketch, in which he casts blackface minstrelsy as a mode of the racial subconscious. Chappelle uses satire and his relationship with his audience as a site of cathartic release by creating "the right kind of laughter": a process where he and his audience collectively acknowledge and engage in the dialectics of an enslaved past and an enduring racist present. The show's failure and Chappelle's departure signify the tension between neoliberal impulses to consume Black satire and Chappelle's desire to control the image, meaning, and laughter of his work.

The third chapter puts Percival Everett's satirical novel *I Am Not Sidney Poitier* in conversation with Sidney Poitier's filmography to highlight the points of departure and negation between the civil rights movement and the post–civil rights moment. Sidney Poitier created a nascent example of Black respectability on the silver screen that Barack Obama later personified in his political career. I argue in the chapter that White male characters were often the site of hostility for Poitier's characters, while White women were often situated as the more progressive voice of reason. The gendered dynamic of white supremacy in these films routinely consumed Poitier's body as a seductive site of racial progress. Everett's main character, Not Sidney, refuses these same sites of consumption and repeatedly diverges from Poitier plotlines to claim more bodily autonomy for himself.

The fourth and final chapter takes up the issue of Black masculine political anger during Obama's presidency. It analyzes race and humor at the White House Correspondents' dinner— specifically Obama's use of the *Key and Peele* character Luther the Anger Translator in 2015 and how the political performance of rage attended to specific moments in Obama's presidency, where he carefully crafted measured responses to racial issues that positioned him as a logical, even-tempered president. Dominant representations of Black masculine anger make a spectacle of Black rage in order to substantiate society's ease with the surveillance and policing of poor Black men while undermining the systemic reasons for their anger. That said, Black men routinely perform anger within this capitalist logic, I argue, as a way of being legible in a broader American (read "White") masculinity, which as Michael Kimmel asserts has become increasingly angry in the twenty-first century. bell hooks's claim that Black male rage is acceptable flattens the reality and representation of many Black men and their nuanced performances and negotiations of anger.

The ubiquity of private expressions and suppressions of Black masculine anger emanate from corporate, political, and academic spaces, and this is well represented in contemporary black satire. "Luther the Anger Translator," wherein they create an imaginative space that can accentuate through the discursive and corporeal translation of the muffled anger and rage behind President Obama's calm and measured affect. The Luther the Anger Translator sketches capture the difficulty and political stakes for the first Black president to publicly perform anger for an angry American citizenry that routinely demands affective performances of its president and sought to appropriate Obama's Black masculine rage.

CHAPTER 1

Of Our Satirical Strivings

JAMES BALDWIN: One of the dangers of being a Black American is being schizophrenic, and I mean "schizophrenic" in the most literal sense. To be a Black American is in some ways to be born with the desire to be white. It's a part of the price you pay for being born here, and it affects every Black person. . . . Du Bois believed in the American dream. So did Martin. So did Malcolm. So do I. So do you. That's why we're sitting here.

AUDRE LORDE: I don't, honey. I'm sorry . . .

THE CONDITION OF blackness in America is a condition of negotiating the hope for a better tomorrow while wrestling with the bleakness of the present. James Baldwin and Audre Lorde's 1984 conversation at Hampshire College in Amherst, Massachusetts, illuminates how the concept of hope is often taken up differently for Black men and women. Baldwin and Lorde's opening meditation on cultural schizophrenia and the desire to be White is a broader conversation about desiring full access to the American Dream. However, their different responses demonstrate how the assemblages of their identity, and specifically their genders, mediate their understanding and proximity to what they consider to be the American Dream. The

American Dream in this context is the desire for social equality and the fullness of American citizenry. Here we should consider how Imani Perry's *Vexy Thing* pushes us to consider how access to the American Dream and citizenship is deeply rooted in historical formations that privilege patriarchy.[1] These formations over time create enduring images and mythologies about who has access to the American Dream.

Baldwin's citing of W.E.B. DuBois, Reverend Martin Luther King Jr., and Malcolm X inadvertently acknowledges the masculinist assumptions about access to the American Dream. Throughout the conversation, Baldwin fails to realize the privileged space from which he speaks as a Black man, and Audre Lorde systematically calls him out for the underlying masculinist assumptions he makes in his commentary about racial uplift. The conversation represents a broader phenomenon in the late twentieth century in racial politics and the rise of Black feminism, with Black men and women arguing who was traumatized more by America's white supremacist heteropatriarchal structure. If hope is an emotional manifestation of the spiritual, political, and social aspirations of variously gendered Black people from antebellum slavery to the present, then the attachment to hope and divergent sites of hope happens differently for Black men and women. For Black men the constitutive power of hope is inured through their proximity to male privilege and a broader embrace of American patriarchy. When Baldwin pathologizes blackness as a schizophrenic desire for whiteness, and then privileges a narrative of racial equality that centers Black men like Du Bois, Martin, and Malcolm thinking along masculine lines to enter into the fullness of American citizenry, he unintentionally limits his view of blackness to Black men. Oppressive regimes afford Black men a conditional form of power over Black women that Black men then misread as provisional sites of equality with White men, and thereby affix it to a broader racial equality for blackness; there has long been an equal opportunity for Black men to oppress

Black women in the same ways that White men have oppressed White women.

From their privileged spaces, Black men have tethered a specific type of political hope to Black existence, thereby creating a dialogic for an ethics of blackness—a moral obligation that requires an unquenchable reservoir of hope be the central defining feature of blackness embodied in the figure of the race man. Baldwin rightly locates Du Bois as an originating architect of the race man as a figure that embodies this political hopefulness to usher in a (Black) American Dream.

Indeed, much of contemporary Black cultural production is invested in the creation, maintenance, and legibility of hope for both Black and White audiences alike. For dominant culture, Black people's hope is marketable. It is palatable. It assuages White guilt and empowers Black people as it reinforces a set of conditions and expectations that suggest that it is unwavering hope that will erode racist structures. These narratives and images of Black hope reinforce what Black intellectuals asserted throughout the twentieth century, that hope is fundamental to racial equality because it victim blames Black people who do not possess this type of hope. From W.E.B. Du Bois's assertion that all art is propaganda "and ever must be" to Cornel West taking to task gangsta rap in *Race Matters* (1993), Black intellectuals have been invested in codifying Black hope as integral to Black liberation. This Black public intellectual tradition has by the same token sought to situate nihilism as anti-Black for the ways it undermines this gendered narrative of hope, while also failing to attend to the role of gender in the intellectual world making and ending that is produced in the discourses of hope-striving and of pessimism and nihilism.

In *The Souls of Black Folk* (1903), Du Bois argues that the perpetual act of "striving" is not just *how* Black people will reach the promised land of racial equality but also *why* they will. It is both the impetus and method for Black intellectual and psychic space that animates Black intellectualism and resistance in the slow march toward social equality.[2] According to Du Bois, "Merely a concrete test of the underlying principles of the great republic is the Negro Problem, and the spiritual striving of the freedmen's sons is the travail of souls whose burden is almost beyond the measure of their strength, but who bear it in the name of an historic race, in the name of this the land of their fathers' fathers, and in the name of human opportunity."[3] Du Bois's emphasis on Black people bearing the "burden" of fighting for racial equality "in the name of human opportunity" lays bare the relationship between striving and racial equality. Du Bois attends to the physical, emotional, and psychological strain of perpetually fighting for racial equality. Du Bois shackles Black humanity to anti-racist work, thereby robbing blackness of its ability to simply exist and thrive without obligation to racial equality.

In *The Souls of Black Folk*, Du Bois oscillates between despair and hope to challenge White American morality and argue for Black equality. Du Bois tethers the emotional undertaking of anti-racist work to a perpetual sense of striving and in so doing creates the terms for Black subjectivity in a Jim Crow America. What is the emotional, psychological, and psychic weight of these strivings? Does the perpetuity of "striving" combat the various structural forms of oppression that are reconstituted throughout the twentieth century, or does it function as an unintended necropolitic that ensures Black and brown women, men, queer-identifying, and disabled people codify exclusive concepts of humanity for marginalized people that is in line with state-sanctioned forms of policing and surveillance?

My aim here is to identify how the perpetuity of a Du Boisian sense of striving sets in motion a definition of Black masculine political performance that associates the laboring (anti-racist) Black body—as the primary site of Black humanity. Second, I want to consider the possibility of Black nihilism as a socio-cultural site of political expression that upends the metric of using the race man to legitimize Black humanity and manhood. Thus, to choose nihilism is a conscious attempt to remove one of the masks of Black masculinity.[4] Indeed, nihilism in the gendered economy of racial uplift functions as an embrace of vulnerability in the ways that it intentionally counters dominant narratives of Black masculine political and intellectual thought. According to Erika Edwards, "It is important to note that the fashioning of black leadership as a distinctly modern trope of normative black masculinity . . . corresponded to the restructuring of the relationship between blacks and the emerging industrial capitalist order after slavery."[5] Edwards's correlation between leadership and capital elucidates the real ways that the Black family structure was implicated in this leadership project. Edwards goes on to articulate how Black subjects use leadership and political agency to combat the continued ways that Black people were disenfranchised and disposed after the abolishment of slavery while simultaneously engaging in a cultural mimesis of "identity and entitlements" that methodically performed a tenuous form of freedom along a broader American cultural logic.

In "Of Our Spiritual Strivings," the first chapter of *Souls*, Du Bois embraces a broader American patriarchy to advance a singular masculine narrative of Black struggle, disillusionment, and despair. Although Du Bois championed women's suffrage and equality, his discursive exclusion of Black women from his articulation of a Black liberationist past, present, and future is persistent throughout the text as he centers Black boys and men in all of his anecdotes and theoretical frameworks.[6] For instance, when Du Bois recounts how he discovered racial inequality as a boy, he asserts that "with other black boys the strife was not so fiercely sunny," and he writes later in the chapter that "the history of the American Negro is the history of this strife—this longing to attain self-conscious manhood."[7] Du Bois's emphasis on other Black boys moves his use of anecdote beyond his personal experience to include only the experiences of boys.

The linkage between self-consciousness and manhood similarly demonstrates a gender-specific articulation of desire and emotions that also prioritize the experiences of Black men. Du Bois follows these instantiations of Black masculine despair and longing with a history of Black struggle that he begins with the enfranchisement of Black men through the passing of the Fifteenth Amendment. Du Bois in this moment, as Hazel Carby argues, sets the terms for the race man as a construct that Black men would perform routinely throughout the twentieth century.[8] Across that century, the race man becomes a sociocultural figure that propagates collective Black political thought and is endowed with charisma and male privilege to advance masculine narratives of racial uplift. This is not to assert that *only* Black men have found themselves able to speak on behalf of "the race." Indeed, scholars like Brittney Cooper's work on race women shows the deep and abiding tradition of Black women leading on conversations about race and racial inequality.[9] However, Black men's national narrative of a "proper," respectable Black masculinity is a masculine performance, which, as Erika Edwards argues, "participates in a gendered economy of political authority in which the attributes of the ideal leader are the traits American society usually conceives as rightly belonging to men or to normative masculinity."[10]

Du Bois's omission of Black women in the first chapter of *Souls* is important for the ways he situates them firmly outside of his conception of his theory of double consciousness. This theory is the centerpiece of "Of Our Spiritual Strivings," so the absence of Black women in these strivings situates them outside of this theoretical framework. If Du Bois had centered or included Black women in his articulation of thinking about Black subjectivity and various ways Black people's existence is mediated by oppressive structures, he would have had to include gender as one of those sites. Du Bois also foregrounds a White male readership at the end of "Of Our Spiritual Striving" when

he writes, "And now what I have briefly sketched in a large outline let me on coming pages tell again in many ways, with loving
emphasis and deeper detail, that men may listen to the striving
in the souls of black folk."[11] With Du Bois's omission of Black
women from the theoretical, anecdotal, and readerly conceptions in *Souls*, his representation of blackness is intrinsically
bound to Black masculinity, thereby making the striving that he
formulates throughout "Of Our Spiritual Striving" an inherently masculine endeavor.

For Du Bois, striving produces an integrationist idyllic state
where Black citizenry and, more specifically, Black manhood,
are actualized through a deep psychological, spiritual, and intellectual effort. As such, Du Bois conceives of Black striving as a
state of being; a critical perspective that undergirded anti-racist
endeavors from the New Negro movement to the civil rights
movement and beyond. Within the framework of being a problem, Du Bois underscores the burden that Blacks share of the
"peculiar sensation" of double consciousness. He uses "Of Our
Spiritual Strivings" to articulate the weight of this twoness that
undergirds his theory of double consciousness. According to Du
Bois, a Black American is one who "ever feels his twoness,—an
American, a Negro; two souls, two thoughts, two unreconciled
strivings; two warring ideals in one dark body, whose dogged
strength alone keeps it from being torn asunder."[12] As one of the
most quoted sections of *Souls* and arguably the conception of
African American studies, Du Bois's use of "striving" both in the
title of the chapter and in his definition of double consciousness
serves as a discursive formation of Black people's psychic yearn-
ings for freedom, with an acknowledgment of the strain that
American racism creates for Black people in their pursuit of
liberation. Although Du Bois outlines that "the end of striving"
as a moment when Black men will "be a co-worker in the kingdom of culture, to escape both death and isolation, to husband and use his best powers and his latent genius," there is a

perpetuity to his sense of striving.[13] Striving as a sociopolitical endeavor necessitates what Paul Gilroy asserts is a politics of fulfillment: "The notion that a future society will be able to realise the social and political promise that present society has left unaccomplished."[14]

The striving that undergirds the race man is the fulcrum of Black political expression throughout the twentieth century and is a culturally specific site of a broader American patriarchy that forecloses for Black women and women more broadly different modes of political action and speech. The organizing ideal of the race man crystallizes throughout the twentieth century and meets the pinnacle of its success during the civil rights movement, with what Robert Patterson refers to as the messianic leadership of Martin Luther King Jr. and others.[15] Under King's tutelage, the civil rights movement further codified the tenets of Black humanity through respectability politics that relied on classism, colorism, sexism, and homophobia to determine ideal representatives and would-be beneficiaries of racial equality. For instance, when the Southern Christian Leadership Conference (SCLC) chose to mobilize around the fairer-complexioned, middle-class Rosa Parks because she embodied a more digestible image of blackness than her darker, younger counterpart Claudette Colvin, who months earlier sat in a Montgomery bus and was similarly arrested, it was intimating that Black people's claims of humanity should be filtered through respectability politics.

The centrality of perpetual striving in Du Bois's configuration of the race man is so deeply entrenched in forms of Black political expression that the absence of these figures in the late twentieth century suggested for Cornel West that nihilism is "the most basic issue now facing black America."[16] For West, nihilism encapsulated a collective emotional, psychological, and spiritual state of crisis for post–civil rights Black subjectivity, in a moment when American racial ideologies were rapidly reimagining themselves into more covert forms of oppression. Nihilism for West is constituted "not as a philosophic doctrine that there are no rational grounds for legitimate standards or authority; it is, far more, the lived experience of coping with a life of horrifying meaninglessness, hopelessness, and (most important) lovelessness."[17] While West notes that the threat of nihilism has been a persistent shadow at the periphery of the experience of Black people in the Americas, one which previous generations found unique psychological, emotional, and spiritual ways to combat, he attributes the contemporary rise in "black nihilism" as a response to the surge of neoliberalism and the "crisis in black leadership."[18]

West's insistence upon a culturally specific site of hope and Black leadership as the ideological underpinning for his articulation of Black nihilism functions beyond the esoteric a priori of academia to articulate a well-established cultural trope of Black political discourse in the late twentieth century. Jesse Jackson's 1988 presidential campaign repackaged these same civil rights ideals for a broader American narrative in his "You Do Not Stand Alone" speech at the 1988 Democratic National Convention (DNC). During the speech, Jackson described his childhood of Black rural poverty as the starting point that led him to the DNC stage and a bid for the White House. He did this to engender a politics of hope, which, as Calvin Warren asserts, "bundles certain promises about redress, equality, freedom, justice, and progress into a political object that always lies beyond reach."[19] As a prominent political and spiritual leader of the civil rights movement, Jackson's beleaguered presidential bid in 1988 situated him as the embodiment of the civil rights striving and hope in the late twentieth century.

Beyond West citing that the "crisis in black leadership" is partially responsible for the rise of nihilism in Black communities, his emphasis on lovelessness, hopelessness, and meaninglessness as the tenets of Black nihilism subtly endorses a Du Boisian sense of striving and insists upon the race man as the sole meaning-making political actor to ground a collective blackness. Blackness's assumed susceptibility to this form of nihilism is a philosophical move that, on the one hand, seemingly colludes with racist ideologies that rob blackness of its humanity by articulating a psychological space that gives way to criminality and, on the other hand, attempts to locate the psychic, mental, economic, and spiritual realities of Black Americans. Nevertheless, West's conception of nihilism is stratified along age and socioeconomic lines that situate the rising threat of nihilism to the poor, Black youth of the 1990s and the dominant discourse of this group as apathetic and violent. West's disregard for a broader conception of nihilism misses the potential of the contemporary moment, and the ways in which many Black subjects in the late twentieth century were increasingly disenchanted with previous efforts toward racial equality.

Whereas West's articulation of nihilism situates blackness in the late twentieth century as lacking substance and direction, Friedrich Nietzsche's use of nihilism argues that life and the metrics that humanity create for it are meaningless because we do not operate from a central concept of truth.[20] West implies that Nietzsche and other philosophers like Martin Heidegger who have theorized the concept of nihilism as the artifice of civilization do not articulate the precarity of Black life in the late twentieth century. Unfortunately, West's ethnocentric definition of nihilism forecloses the possibility of reconstituting late twentieth-century Black disillusionment as a positive and necessary development in Black subjectivity. My use of "disillusionment" here on the one hand acknowledges the continued dialectic between Black subjectivity and subjugation that affords Black people a psychological durability for negotiating an increasingly imaginative, white supremacist culture in the present moment. On the other hand, my use of it is attuned to how it is a necessary part of critique and evolution in social justice spaces. Presumably West recognizes the important role of a broader philosophical understanding of nihilism in *Race Matters*. According to him, "The first African encounter with the New World was an encounter with a distinctive form of the Absurd. The initial Black struggle against degradation and devaluation in the enslaved circumstances of the New World was, in part, a struggle against nihilism."[21] However, according to Nietzsche, "because the values we have had hitherto thus draw their final consequence; because nihilism represents the ultimate logical conclusion of our great values and ideals—because we must experience nihilism before we can find out what value these 'values' really had. We require, sometime, *new values*."[22]

To embrace nihilism is to embrace vulnerability and the broad ways it asks us to depart from value systems that make sense of the world around us. To embrace nihilism is to supplant structure with chaos toward the potential of something new. For Black masculinity, the embrace of nihilism has the potential to function as the necessary death of a cadre of patriarchal formations, including our collective reliance on messianic Black male leadership. Within the figurative death of the race man, inactivity becomes activity, and being apolitical becomes radically political.

Whereas Du Bois intentionally creates the framework for the race man as an important interlocutor in the problem of the twentieth century, Paul Beatty, a novelist whose work spans the end of the twentieth century and the beginning of the twenty-first, demonstrates the enduring reality of racism for Black people and attempts to liberate Black masculinity, and a broader Black subjectivity, from the failed promise of the race man by embracing nihilism. Like Beatty's three previous novels, *The Sellout* (2015) is a first-person narrative that nihilistically explores the fictive boundaries of blackness by creating the terms for an unlikely race man to do "race work."[23] Beatty's novel echoes his sentiment that "my resentment has become so overbearing that these days I'm unable to take anything seriously, much less humorously. Everything is satirical. Not *Mad* magazine satirical but Orwellian dystopic."[24] *The Sellout* follows an unnamed protagonist—a young, Black horticulturalist—through the rise and fall of his becoming a twenty-first-century slave owner and segregation enthusiast. He sacrilegiously re-creates the terms of enslavement and segregation as a form of (Black) community building in Dickens, a city within the greater Los Angeles area. As he proclaims, "I'm a farmer: we segregate in an effort to give every tree, every plant, every poor Mexican, every poor nigger, a chance for equal access to sunlight and water; we make sure every living organism has room to breathe" (214). Beatty's protagonist uses farming as a humorous and apt metaphor for equity to argue for strategy-based interventions for people of color.

In this way, Beatty employs irony as a post-soul satirical tool to create a radical Black masculine subjectivity that liberates Black subjects, specifically Black men, from incessant racial striving by rupturing the cultural veneer of the race man.[25] Beatty provides alternatives to the striving race man throughout his work. For instance, his first novel, *The White Boy Shuffle* (1996), the protagonist begins by stating, "Unlike the typical bluesy earthy folksy denim-overalls noble-in-the-face-of-cracker-racism aw shucks Pulitzer Prize–winning protagonist mojo magic Black man, I am not the seventh son of a seventh son of a seventh son" (5).[26] At first glance, the protagonist's assertion seemingly counters the literary tradition of Zora Neale Hurston, Alice Walker, and Toni Morrison, whose rustic depictions of Black Southern life tend to speak to the resilience of blackness during Jim Crow racism and often contain a supernatural element. While I do not discount that Beatty is pivoting on the well-established literary representation of blackness and Black masculinity in Black women's literature, he is also speaking directly to W.E.B. Du Bois in this passage. In *Souls*, Du Bois writes that "after the Egyptian and Indian, the Greek and Roman, the Teuton and Mongolian, the Negro is a sort of seventh son, born with a veil, and gifted with second-sight in this American world."[27] Du Bois's articulation of a supernatural second sight of oppressed people is embedded in his use of the folkloristic trope of the seventh son and falls in line with his focus on Black men throughout *Souls*. Beatty's *White Boy Shuffle*, like his subsequent novels, is by contrast a literary exploration in imagining Black masculinity beyond the confines of a racial striving politics, and as such creates a resistant depiction of Black masculine performances that should be studied in this contemporary moment.

Beatty's use of irony and subversion in his counternarratives is a palimpsest of the civil rights imaginary; an imaginary, I argue, where a Du Boisian sense of striving colludes with respectability politics to form the mythos for a contemporary Black critical consciousness.[28] Stated differently, the national nostalgia and legacy of the civil rights movement concretizes the race man as the ideal leader and nonviolent protest as the sole means of implementing social justice work. Throughout *The Sellout*, Beatty pivots around these highly visual, static moments of the civil rights movement to ask whether it was worth it. "Most people," Beatty states in an interview, "think that it's been worth it—I mean, obviously it has—but we don't know how to measure that."[29] Beatty uses irony as a satirical tool to subvert the significance of highly visual civil rights moments—like the picture of Rosa Parks sitting in the bus seat, or Emmett Till's face in *Jet* magazine. "These images," according to Nicole Fleetwood, "serve as one of the primary modes in which the fight for civil rights and equality gets understood and memorialized in dominant discourse and public culture."[30] For dominant culture, as Fleetwood argues, these images become a way to historicize, distance, and commodify an overtly racist past from a contemporary national narrative of progress. Beatty's post–civil rights palimpsests are important for the ways they intervene in this national narrative of progress. For Beatty, subverting the underlying narrative behind these iconic images figuratively ends their representation of perpetual striving and reappropriates them in order to encompass the everyday absurdities of Black life.

Beatty creates two types of civil rights palimpsest throughout *The Sellout*. The first is a type of historical musing that imagines an alternative civil rights psyche that shifts the terms of anti-racist work during the period. In this type of palimpsest, Beatty returns to the precise moment of civil rights work; the moment when Rosa Parks refuses her seat, or Martin Luther King is at the podium on the National Mall in Washington, DC, in order to replace these civil rights icons' ostensible sense of striving with absurdity and nihilism. For instance, when the protagonist daydreams early in the novel that "the marchers on Washington become civil rights zombies. . . . The head zombie looks exhausted. . . . He doesn't know the mic is on, and under his breath he confesses that if he'd only tasted the unsweetened swill that passed for iced tea at the segregation lunch counters in the South he would've called the whole civil rights thing off. Before the boycotts, the beatings, and the killings" (19). Here, King delivering his "I Have a Dream" speech on the steps of the Lincoln Memorial before the multitudes is arguably the most circulated image of the time, and as such, is an image and speech that embodies perpetual striving. By using zombies in this passage, Beatty intimates that civil rights icons are continually resurrected, oftentimes against their will, to typify the longitudinal boundaries of blackness. As a civil rights palimpsest, Beatty humorously subverts one of the most significant moments during the civil rights movement—and the most important in its legacy—to illuminate the potential futility of striving to question if integration was worth "the boycotts, the beatings, and the killings"—and nasty tea. The unsweetened tea is humorous because it understates the reason for integration while also working as a metaphor to question the desire for integration.

Beatty begins his justification for a post–civil rights resegregation of Dickens by revisiting the iconic image of Rosa Parks

sitting in the front of a Montgomery bus. Sparked by Hominy
Jenkins giving up his seat to a White woman—and thinking it
potentially had less to do with her whiteness and more to do
with her attractiveness, the protagonist thinks, "That notion had
me reassessing the entire civil rights movement. Maybe race had
nothing to do with it" (133). While the statement seems innocu-
ous, Beatty's protagonist imagines a Jim Crow history that
detaches the centrality of race from the civil right movement.
Beatty then imagines a Jim Crow past that pivots less on racial
difference and is instead propelled by avoiding mundane annoy-
ances: "So like those high school white girls who have after-
school sex with the burly black athlete in the wood shop, and
then cry rape when their fathers find out, maybe Rosa Parks,
after the arrest, the endless church rallies, and all the press, had
to cry racism, because what was she going to say: 'I refused to
move because the man asked me what I was reading'? Negroes
would've lynched her" (133–134). By comparing Parks's situation with a White girl that lies about being raped by a Black boy,
Beatty irreverently illustrates how race can serve as a coercive
hermeneutic that necessitates a race-based reading of the world.

Furthermore, Beatty's use of an image of a White girl and
the discourse of rape in his historical and cultural revisionist
work of Parks illustrates the extent to which he wants to trouble
contemporary integrationist logic. Beatty links the Jim Crow era
to the post–civil rights moment by creating a continuum from
an era of unfettered lynching to contemporary Black masculine
precarity caused by similarly untrue claims of Black rape. Such
integrationist logic holds that, with the end of de jure racism,
disparities in education, mass incarceration, and housing, for
example, became nonexistent. The Emancipation Proclamation
and the Civil Rights Act did not eradicate institutions of white
supremacy and racism. Instead, these sites of racial oppression
simply evolved and maintain their legacy of dispossession and
dehumanization. Thus, the myth of Black men's insatiable sexual

appetites that informed early Black codes on plantations and postbellum miscegenation laws is just as relevant today.

PICAROS PUTTING THE "POST" IN POST–CIVIL RIGHTS

Beatty writes *The Sellout* in the neopicaresque tradition, one that relies on irony and helps to create the terms for his second type of civil rights palimpsest. The picaresque novel originated in seventeenth-century Spain as a genre that featured its "picaro," the novel's protagonist or hero, who episodically negotiates his outsider status in society to critique the social and political flaws of mankind. In *The Myth of the Picaro*, Alexander Blackburn elucidates the somewhat overlapping relationship between the picaresque tradition and satire when he writes, "Whereas it might be said that formal satire dissolves reality with reference to the satirist's chosen norms, it might also be said that picaresque satire makes dissolution eventful, a psychological loss of the picaro's sense of reality during his entanglement with his world."[31] Blackburn demonstrates how satire flattens characters to create the terms for critique and adds that satires that rely on the picaresque tradition do so to create more nuanced characters that provide the interiority necessary for a more emotional and psychological satirical critique.

Contemporary Black satirical novels are patterned after the old Spanish picaresque tradition. According to Darryl Dickson-Carr, "The picaresque story, then, is frequently an ironic commentary upon the problematic acceptability of subversive or transgressive behavior at a time when the cultural politics of a society are in a state of flux or relative uncertainty."[32] After the conservative turn in the 1980s, it was the early 1990s that witnessed an intentional, albeit reluctant, engagement with civil rights legislation to construct the national narrative of multiculturalism. Since this moment, I argue, race and gender have broadly been in a state of flux as the nation grapples with tolerance and inclusivity of marginalized groups. According to

Blackburn, "The fundamental situation of the literary picaro is the loneliness of an individual isolated *within* society....The picaro's loneliness is by contrast the outgrowth of the sense of failed identity, of the instability of an inferior social standing, and of the failure to find human solidarity."[33] Since blackness, like gender identity, is overdetermined in this country, the picaro's isolation and "failed identity" are advantageous to the satirist's desire to question how the prevailing definitions of blackness often preclude many Black Americans.

For contemporary Black visual and literary satirists such as Percival Everett, Spike Lee, Paul Beatty, Aaron McGruder, and Matt Johnson, the picaro enters into their Black satirical landscapes for the ways he capitalizes on America's ever-evolving racial and gender landscape.[34] Black satirists use of this form dates to Ralph Ellison's *Invisible Man* (1953), and while the picaro serves as an exemplar for a postwar, postmodernist sensibility, this contemporary moment further elucidates the potential of this literary outsider to comment upon the postracial mythos of the twenty-first century. I want to pause for a moment to think about the relational sense of vulnerability that the picaro creates for Black masculine characters in satire.

As critical outsider, the picaro in contemporary satire inhabits a vulnerable subjectivity through his lack of community. Judith Butler asserts that it is our interdependency that produces the precarity embedded in our collective human condition and that renders us all vulnerable.[35] However, in Black cultural production, literary and otherwise, community and the sense of belonging have been central in the creation and maintenance of radical Black subjectivities. Toni Morrison, Alice Walker, and others center community and belonging as staples of a "healthy" Black literary subjectivity—one where a sense of home, self, and community helps to maintain emotional, psychological, and physical safety of Black characters. It is from this ontological space that the Black picaro in contemporary satire creates a site of vulnerability through his intentional refusal of a physical community coupled with his ideological underpinnings that run counter to popular representations of blackness. The Black picaro's vulnerability is one caused by his isolated nature and not his relationship to others.

The Sellout enters the picaresque tradition in the ways in which Dickens and its inhabitants readily return to de jure racism during a seemingly postracial moment—as such, the commentary that Beatty makes about Dickens is a microcosm of our current "postracial" America. Beatty's unnamed protagonist is a picaro for the ways he functions as "the quintessential African American satiric figure insofar as he seeks the bridges between two worlds, the heroic and the ironic."[36]

By establishing the permanency of the picaresque tradition and specifically the role of the picaro in contemporary Black satire, I argue the tenor of contemporary revisionist work embedded in Beatty's and other contemporary satirists' palimpsests represents a tonal shift from striving to absurdity. According to Beatty in an early interview, in his writing he tries to "be vulnerable and not afraid to parody things that are important to you and to others.... In real life, the antihero wins and does the right thing just as much as the hero."[37] Although Beatty does not use "picaro" by name, his use of "antihero" and his investment in vulnerability illuminates his intent to create protagonists and narratives that move beyond the heroic.

Beatty's second type of palimpsest situates his picaro in the contemporary revision of civil rights narratives. For instance, Beatty tacitly evokes the story of Emmett Till as a way to demonstrate unbridled racism. Beatty uses the story to demonstrate the impossibility of re-creating moments of Jim Crow racial terror in the post–civil rights era. Emmett Till was a fourteen-year-old boy from Chicago visiting his grandfather in Money, Mississippi, in the summer of 1955. It was long held as fact that Till whistled at Carolyn Bryant, a White woman, at a small grocery store that she and her husband owned in town. However, Carolyn later said that she lied about the interaction and that Till did not whistle at her.[38] A few nights after Till's non-whistle, Carolyn's husband Roy Bryant and friend J. W. Milam took Till at gunpoint from his grandfather's house in the middle of night. For the next day, they relentlessly beat, dismembered, and shot him. They then tied his body to a cotton gin and threw it in the Tallahatchie River. The sheriff quickly tried to have the body buried but Emmett's mother, Mamie Till, said "she wanted 'all the world' to witness the atrocity."[39] Beatty intentionally complicates the assumed singularity and static nature of history when he writes in *The Sellout*, "That's the problem with history, we like to think it's a book—that we can turn the page and move the fuck on. But history isn't the paper it's printed on. It's memory, and memory is time, emotions, and song. History is the things that stay with you" (115). *The Sellout*, like most post-soul endeavors, becomes a way to unhinge historical certainty by reshaping a collective past to elucidate present sensibilities.

Like the story of Rosa Parks on the bus in Montgomery, Emmett Till's story is one of the civil rights movement's most sacrosanct moments because of the ways that it helped to stimulate and immobilize a movement into national existence, and Beatty's continues his sacrilegious treatment here. Beatty's narrative style is as important as what happens, so I will quote at length here. The protagonist states, "One day I foolishly said to my father that there was no racism in America. Only equal opportunity that black people kick aside because we don't want to take responsibility for ourselves" (174). Later that evening, "he [his father] snatched me up out of bed, and together we took an ill-prepared cross-country trip into deepest, whitest America. . . . We ended up in a nameless Mississippi town that was nothing more than a dusty intersection of searing heat, crows, cotton fields, and, judging by the excited look of anticipation on my father's face, unadulterated racism" (174). The protagonist's father drives across the country with the sole purpose of having his son whistle at a White woman working as a store clerk. Ultimately, his son fails because "whistling is one of the few things you learn at public school" and the protagonist is homeschooled. Frustrated, the father "pursed his lips and let go a wolf whistle so lecherous and libidinous it curled both the white woman's pretty painted toes and the dainty red ribbon in her blond hair. Now it was her turn, and my father stood there lustful and black, as she just as defiantly not only recklessly eyeballed him back but recklessly rubbed his dick through his pants" (177). The scene ends with the father leaving the general store with the White store clerk to have sex, with his son left to draw his own conclusions about the state of race and racism.

Beatty's palimpsest between Till and the protagonist advances a subtle gendered critique of Black masculine sexuality in the historical racial violence that he promulgates. In the summer of 1955, the tenets of Jim Crow rendered Till's act of whistling illicit as a convergence of racial and sexual misconduct. As a Black boy visiting the South, Till was seemingly unaware of the myth of the Black male rapist and the history of Black men being lynched because of their sexual proximity to White women. Beatty's palimpsest demonstrates that Black men's sexuality is no longer repudiated in the same ways that it once was. For instance, one of the White men watching the above scene unfold asks, "Is there a black buck Rebecca ain't fucked from here to Natchez?," and another retorts, "Well, least she knows what she likes. Your dumb peckerwood ass still ain't decided whether you like men or not" (177). The humor is undeniable, as their acceptance of the White woman's preference for Black men gives way to a broader progressiveness about queer sexuality—even as it mocks one of the friends for either his bisexuality or sexual curiosity. The shift in the narrative and the break from history suggests that the politics around Black men's sexuality are not as regressive as they were in 1955.

In addition to the specificity of these civil rights palimpsests, Beatty engages a broader civil rights ethos earlier in the novel that sets the terms of his post–civil rights revisionism. In the novel's prologue, when the protagonist is sitting in the Supreme Court being tried for breaking the Thirteenth and Fourteenth Amendments, he thinks:

Uncomfortable with being so comfortable, I make one last attempt to be at one with my people. I close my eyes, place my head on the table, and bury my nose in the crook of my arm. I focus on my breathing, shutting out the flags and the fanfare, and cull through my vast repository of daydream blackness until I dredge up the scratchy archival footage of the civil rights struggle. Handling it carefully by its sensitive edges, I remove it from its sacred canister, thread it through mental sprockets and psychological gates, and past the bulb in my head that flickers with the occasional decent idea. I flip on the projector. There's no need to focus. Human carnage is always filmed and remembered in the highest definition. The images are crystal-clear, permanently burned into our memoires and plasma television screens. That incessant Black History Month loop of barking dogs, gushing fire hoses, and carbuncles oozing blood through two-dollar haircuts, colorless blood spilling down faces shiny with sweat and the light of the evening news, these are the pictures that form our collective 16mm superego. . . . The film inside my head begins to skip and sputter. The sound cuts out, and protesters falling like dominoes in Selma, Alabama, begin to look like Keystone Negroes slipping en masse on an affirmative-action banana peel and tumbling to the street, a tangled mess of legs and dreams akimbo. . . . Still, I don't feel guilty. If I'm indeed moving backward and dragging all of black America down with me, I couldn't care less. (18–19)

The sepia tint through which Beatty views civil rights iconography represents a psychological process that establishes the permanency of a "conscious" Black subjectivity. It intimates that the static imagery of the civil rights movement creates with its barking dogs and water hoses a Black ontological space for a contemporary Black subject formation. The protagonist's inability to enter the psychic space of contemporary Black "consciousness" and its reliance on comfortability as the filter through which blackness is mediated, authenticated, and performed, suggests that previous ways of being no longer serve as the paragon for Black life. In other words, in articulating the ontology that civil rights iconography is supposed to produce, the protagonist represents the frailty of these images by portraying them as part of an untended and diminishing archive.

In the passage above, Beatty articulates one of many sites of emotionality for post-soul blackness. The interplay between a tacitly recognized site of racial guilt and the comfort and freedom of not being burdened by acknowledging its presence and at the same time not feeling it as signifiers of the extent to which blackness is overdetermined by civil rights. "I, too, keep waiting for that familiar, overwhelming sense of Black guilt to drop me to my knees. Knock me down peg by meaningless idiomatic peg, until I'm bent over in total supplication to America, tearfully confessing my sins against color and country, begging my proud black history for forgiveness. But there's nothing" (17).

COMMUNAL SELF-CARE AND NIGGER WHISPERING

In addition to the vulnerability of the picaro, Beatty uses the themes of suicide and mental health to depict Black precarity and demonstrate the mental and psychological toll of an integrationist logic in an unapologetically racist society. In *The Sellout*, the protagonist's father is known as the "Nigger Whisperer" for the ways he has helped citizens on the brink of suicide. As a trope of anti-racist work and community building, suicide serves as a construct for the outsider negotiating blackness both in this novel and *The White Boy Shuffle*. The latter is a satirical picaresque novel about protagonist Gunnar Kaufman and his negotiation of Black authenticity, masculinity, and the idea of racial uplift during the 1990s in Southern California and Boston. Gunnar is a basketball-playing, "urban folk" poet "preordained by a set of weak-kneed DNA to shuffle in the footsteps of a long cowardly queue of coons, Uncle Toms, and faithful boogedy-boogedy retainers" before being thrust into the role of Messianic race man (5). His contribution to anti-racist activism in the late twentieth century is to ask Blacks to make a suicide pact because "past movements in the black struggle seem to have had the staying power of an asthmatic marathoner with no sense of direction, so I suppose as movements go, this one is better than most" (225).

Similar to *The Sellout*, *White Boy Shuffle* pivots around the civil rights movement, and Gunnar proposes suicide through an adaptation of a King quote: "If a man hasn't discovered something he will die for, he isn't fit to live" (200). Gunnar uses this as the theoretical underpinning for his call for a mass suicide pact. He breaks down the logic of anti-racist suicide work thus: "So I asked myself, what am I willing to die for. The day when white people treat me with respect and see my life as equally valuable to theirs. No, I ain't willing to die for that, because if they don't know that by now, then they ain't never going to know it. Matter of fact, I ain't ready to die for anything, so I guess I'm just not fit to live. In other words, I'm just ready to die. I'm just ready to die" (200). Gunnar's use of King's words helps him to create a post-soul, post–civil rights dialectic for understanding the morbidity of the present moment through the continued presence of American racism. Ironically, Gunnar's lack of a cause to commit to gives him a cause to both live *and* die for. As the novel ends, and suicide letters in the form of poems start

to get sent to Gunnar, the reader is left contemplating the play-
fulness of Beatty's message. Gunnar is asked at one point about
mass suicide being an indicator that Black people have given
up—to which he responds, "That's the Western idea of suicide—
the sense of the defeated self. 'Oh, the dysfunctional people
couldn't adjust to our great system, so they killed themselves.' . . .
It is as Mishima once said: 'Sometimes hara-kiri [another name
for seppuku] makes you win.' I just want to win one time" (202).
He is then asked, "Last laugh?" "I don't see anyone laughing," he
replies (202). Gunnar's failure to situate this as a laughing matter
calls into question the seriousness of his proposal.

Whereas in *White Boy Shuffle* Beatty morbidly asserts that
suicide serves as the ultimate escapism and thereby solution to
American racism, in *The Sellout* he shifts his treatment of suicide
to reconstitute it as a by-product of living in the American racial
landscape where Black people negotiate society's consumption
of Black bodies. According to the protagonist, "In the years after
my father died, the neighborhood looked to me to be the next
Nigger Whisperer. I wish I could say that I answered the call to
duty out of a sense of familial pride and communal concern, but
the truth was, I did it because I had no social life" (58). The protagonist's apathy toward his "whispering" reifies his positionality
as an antihero in order to reject his potential configuration as a
hero and a race man. In this section of the novel, the protagonist
differentiates himself from his father who is compelled by "communal concern" and a greater sense of "striving" to render the
reason for his service ridiculous.

Beatty's protagonist haplessly falls into owning a slave when
his elderly friend, Hominy Jenkins, a former child star on Hal
Roach's *Our Gang*, feels indebted to the protagonist because he
stops Hominy from committing suicide. In a failed attempt to
demonstrate his indebtedness, Hominy enslaves himself. "True
freedom," Hominy says, "is having the right to be a slave. . . .
I know taint nobody forcin' me, but dis here one slave you ain't

never gwine be rid of. Freedom can kiss my postbellum black ass" (83). There is an ironic truth in what Hominy says about the choice to be enslaved. Indeed, the relationship that Hominy creates with the protagonist is a purely performative experience of enslavement because the concept of choice makes their arrangement something other than slavery. Hominy is an absurd character throughout the novel. "Hominy" evokes the porter figure on the Cream of Wheat boxes and "Jenkins" is arguably one of the Blackest surnames. His character is an embodiment of caricature—someone whose existence is confirmed through his proximity to stereotypes. The protagonist's commitment to Hominy's happiness drives the plot of the novel by reinstituting segregation in Dickens, "The Last Bastian of Blackness," an all-Black and Latino community in the Los Angeles area that is fighting for visibility after it is literally taken off the map (150).

The psychological elements of the novel become more explicit toward its end. In the acknowledgments section Beatty thanks and references William E. Cross Jr.'s "The Negro-to-Black Conversion Experience" (1971), an article that he "read in grad school and has stayed with me ever since."[40] Cross's text serves as the theoretical backbone for the strata of blackness that the protagonist rearticulates at the end of the novel and that Beatty extends by including "Unmitigated Blackness." "Unmitigated Blackness," the protagonist says, "is a seeming unwillingness to succeed," later adding that it "is a coming to the realization that as fucked up and meaningless as it all is, sometimes it's the nihilism that makes life worth living" (277). As such, Unmitigated Blackness is the novel's articulation of an ideal post-soul subjectivity—a site of blackness that recognizes the racial dialectic between stereotypes and subsequent modalities of Black existence that are continuously created and re-created to better help Black people negotiate global anti-blackness. Cross's initial stratification of blackness comprises five stages: Pre-Encounter, Encounter, Immersion-Emersion, Internalization, and Commitment. Cross's stages articulate the psychology behind Black people's embrace of blackness at different evolutionary stages. The pinnacle of Cross's model, which is commonly referred to as the Cross Racial Identity Scale, situates the most evolved form of blackness as Commitment. This form of blackness is invested in embodying blackness in a way that moves beyond the visual markers of material objects like that of a Black Power fist, Afro pick, or clothes sporting pithy sayings and civil rights icons to one that is coupled with a commitment to bettering in some way the realities of Black folks. Unfortunately, Cross makes a similar mistake to Du Bois by linking one's blackness to one's ability to attend to the racist structures undergirding the Black experience. According to Cross, "The individual functioning at the fifth stage differs from the person in the fourth stage in that he or she is committed to a plan. He is actively trying to change his community. . . . He is going beyond rhetoric and into action and he defines change in terms of the masses of Black people rather than the advancement of a few."[41] Cross's suggestion that the highest form of blackness requires a plan, and I would add a level of nuance, implies an ability to move in a White world to belie the freedom associated with being outside a purely resistant and reactionary form of blackness that is always responding to White oppression. The plan that Cross outlines in his fifth stage requires an investment in the communal and has historically been a space in which respectability politics and other forms and practices of blackness have been adopted in order to ensure the success of any plan towards racial progress.

Unmitigated Blackness differs from Cross's last stage to assert that Black subjects do not need a plan of communal uplift in order to achieve a heightened level of blackness. Instead, in Beatty's articulation, Black subjects reach a higher state of blackness—an *unmitigated* state—by inhabiting a painful satire; a type of bleak sarcasm that requires an acknowledgment of the effects of oppressive structures and a decision to defiantly resist the integrationist logic of respectability that dictates Black subjects avoid stereotypes at all cost, thereby allowing them to embrace stereotypical acts but not the racist logic behind them. Beatty draws this logic to its absurd conclusion by having his protagonist segregate a community of color from a nonpresent White population. In this way, Beatty troubles our collective understanding of the figure of the racial "sellout" due in part to its reliance on the overdetermination of blackness in order to illuminate the ways in which this figure can be liberated from the weight of "properly" performing blackness. Characters like Derrick Bell's Dr. Golightly in his short story "Space Traders" (1992), the protagonist of Sam Greenlee's novel *The Spoke Who Sat by the Door* (1969), Raven Quickskill in Ishmael Reed's novel *Flight to Canada* (1976), and Pierre Delacroix in Spike Lee's film *Bamboozled* (2000) embody the ease with which Black people and specifically Black men embrace the figure of the sellout.[42] Whereas these characters embrace the role of the sellout in order to gain access and ultimately sabotage conservative political and corporate regimes invested in the surveillance and disenfranchisement of Black people, Unmitigated Blackness is less concerned with this type of subversiveness and more invested in laying bare racial formations and assumptions by refusing to engage them.

By novel's end Blackness is no longer tethered to respectability politics and the desire to be legible to a broader American public through its endless commitment to ending racial violence and inequality. As Lisa Guerrero reminds us, "Finding worth in meaninglessness (instead of finding despair in it), requires an astute talent for improvisation."[43] While Guerrero argues that this larger improvisation is found in places that might be considered nontraditional sties of Blackness, it is important to think through what meaninglessness and inaction would mean for the Race man and the gendered dynamics of racial uplift. Ultimately, Unmitigated Blackness reckons with the enduring legacy of racism. Whereas striving and the respectability politics of the race man suggest that the end to racism is always close at hand but just out of reach, Unmitigated Blackness is invested in a communal, self-care project that asks that blackness look beyond anti-racism as a defining tool for its humanity. Unmitigated Blackness is thus an endorsement of nihilism as a way to create space to question the political impetus behind the race man, and to think imaginatively about new, more inclusive modes of Black political life that do not link Black humanity to race work.

CHAPTER 2

Neoliberalism and the Funny Race Man

IN CHAPTER 1, I argued that a momentary turn to nihilism is an apt approach for Black men to turn away from the race man figure. In this chapter, I will continue to think about the elisions between satirists and satire and how the terms of the contemporary funny race man shift for sketch comedy. There is a connectedness and kinship between satirists and their work. Satirists have a proclivity to reproduce a version of themselves in their satires. This phenomenon is in part due to the ways that satirists have to re-create the world and its social ills—namely assumptions and stereotypes about race and blackness in the case of Black satirists. Thus, Percival Everett puts a Professor Everett in his novel *I Am Not Sidney Poitier* (discussed in chapter 3). There are similarities between Paul Beatty and Gunnar Kaufman, the protagonist of *The White Boy Shuffle*, that are beyond coincidental—both are from Southern California, write poetry, and attend Boston University. This is part due to the way that contemporary cultural production is invested in the individual and part due to the need to put into the narrative landscape the satirist's sensibilities as a necessary intervention or site of critique. My turn to Dave Chappelle in this chapter as both satirist and character in his sketches acknowledges the slippages between reality and satirical critique idea of the race man in neoliberal markets.

Dave Chappelle, like most Black comedians, primarily leverages authenticity and authority in his ability to speak broadly
about race and racism in his stand-up routines. Due to the short
interaction between comedian and audience, I situate Black
sketch comedy as a site of what Wahneema Lubiano refers to as
"Black common sense."[1] These are examples, albeit funny ones, of
a Black nationalist logic. This logic centers cisgender, heterosexual
Black men as patriarchs of the Black family and de facto leaders
of Black liberation movements. For comedians, Black common
sense allows them to offer up remixed platitudes of Black hard-
ship, sacrifice, and resilience as a way to strengthen Black communities, oftentimes at the expense of Black women and queer
folxs. Black queer scholars have gone to great lengths to show
how Black common sense relies on hegemonic forms of Black
masculinity. Scholars like Marlon Riggs, E. Patrick Johnson, and
others demonstrate that it is the "humor" of comedians like Eddie
Murphy, the "Men on Film" sketches in *In Living Color*, as well as
other sites of Black masculinity that leverages the authenticity and
authority of Black common sense to create the boundaries of
Black masculinity and by extension blackness.[2] Black men are
able to achieve the hypervisibility of the Black funny man by
relying on Black common sense for the ways that this strategic
nationalist image is cis-gendered and heteropatriarchal.

When we consider the short time frame for sketch comedy,
the reliance on Black common sense is even more exaggerated in
these spaces. In *Sketch Comedy: Identity, Reflexivity, and American
Television*, Nick Marx asserts that sketch comedy relies on a
reflexive/ flexibility framework, a process by which sketch comedies incorporate a kind of meta commentary about the comedic
process that also leaves space for fluidity in how and what it critiques.[3] To extend Marx's critique, both the reflexive and flexible
possibilities of Black sketch comedy reside in their ability to use
Black nationalistic frameworks and concepts as touchstones for

the cultural commentary and artistic process they are engaging in. There are slippages between satirists, their satire, and their reliance on Black common sense as an underlying ethos for the kinds of social, cultural, and political commentaries offered up in these spaces.

Continuing the tradition of *The Richard Pryor Show* (1977), *In Living Color* (1990–1994), and, to a lesser extent, *The Chris Rock Show* (1997–2000), *Chappelle's Show* (2003–2006) features a highly visible young Black man who is a humorous interlocutor in national conversations about race and racism. Comedy Central's website still touts it as a "social phenomenon."[4] Like his predecessors, Chappelle came to sketch comedy by way of a successful stand-up career, as well as through his cult classic film *Half Baked* (1998).[5] However, he did not become a juggernaut of Black popular culture until he performed Black authenticity in more legibly "cool" ways—what Bambi Haggins terms the "multiple levels of 'down-ness.'"[6]

Taped in front of a studio audience, the sketches for *Chappelle's Show* were prerecorded and then replayed in a lounge-like atmosphere. With an average of more than 3 million viewers each episode, the show became a television event. People all around the country were talking and laughing about race. Yet Comedy Central's ability to monetize Chappelle's biting critiques of American racism and thereby reproduce a system of control that his satire sought to critique complicated the comedian's relationship to his work. His last sketch on the show, "The Nigger Pixie," is a particularly powerful illustration of how the emotional, psychological, and economic toll of a network pushing him to inhabit the role of the modern-day race man mediated Chappelle's artistic freedom and his ability to critique racism.

Early in Dave Chappelle's career his Black masculine performance was in the countercultural space between Black nerd culture and drug culture. His persona, as Haggins asserts, wasn't the embodiment of Black masculine cool like many of his ante-cedents'. Prior to Chappelle, socially progressive Black comedi-ans that pushed issues around race in their stand-up routines all embodied coolness as a central part of their onstage persona. In many ways, these comedic juggernauts were personifications of the cool pose—a calm, emotionless, and fearless façade whose emotional detachment is matched only by their suaveness. Chap-pelle, unlike Eddie Murphy, did not wear leather on the stand-up stage. He did not exhibit the cool suaveness that usually accompa-nied Black masculine comedic performances. Historically, the lack of this coolness meant that you were a physical comedian more focused on corporeality and spastic movement. There is a long history of Black physical comedians and the slippery slope that gets back to the minstrel stage as a primarily physical come-dic space, but Chappelle did not take up this site of Black mas-culine performance for his persona. Instead, he created a space of Black masculine awkwardness that was largely unto itself and that seems to have been an organizing ethos for the likes of Keegan-Michael Key, Jordan Peele, Hannibal Buress, Michael Che, and others. Chappelle was able to be the awkward, skinny Black guy and partake in counterculture without it affecting his proximity to blackness because of his relationship to socially conscious rap and neo-soul.

For Chappelle, it was his close proximity to conscious rappers like Mos Def and neo-soul artists like Erykah Badu that grounded his Black authenticity and authority and by extension the authen-ticity of the show. With Chappelle functioning as a purveyor of subculture, these socially conscious rappers and neo-soul singers routinely performed and made cameos on his television show. During the late 1990s and early 2000s, neo-soul emerged as a subgenre of hip-hop that blends rap and rhythm and blues. As an evolution of conscious rap, neo-soul blended Black nationalist sensibilities with sonic formations of soul and funk to critique racist and capitalistic structures in Black communities in the late twentieth century. Artists such as Common Sense, Jill Scott, The Roots, Erykah Badu, Indie Arie, Musiq Soulchild, D'Angelo, and others are firmly situated in the neo-soul tradition. These artists make music that highlights Black life, love, community, and a connection to nature. With clear roots in earlier soul, neo-soul was a clear departure from some of the harder performances of commercially successful hip-hop in the mid- to late 1990s.

Rappers like Ice Cube, Tupac Shakur, Biggie Smalls and others had popularized gangsta rap in the years preceding the explosion of neo-soul in hip-hop spaces. Gritty hardness, urban decay, poverty, and incarceration were all popular themes of gangsta rap that were brought into the mainstream as a way to annunciate mass incarceration, the prison industrial complex, and the effects of Reagan's war on drugs and Clinton's Violent Crime Control and Law Enforcement Act in 1994. Neo-soul then enters into the hip-hop landscape of the late 1990s as an intervention of Black social and political performances and discourses to help show the fullness of Black life. For Chappelle, this brand of blackness resonated with his comedic persona for the ways that it was both unapologetically Black and at the same time alternative in that it was not commercialized.

POST-SOUL LAUGHTER

In 2006, as part of the Sundance Institute's interview series *Iconoclast*, Dave Chappelle spoke with Maya Angelou. Explaining that his satirical work is personal and "when done well, cathartic," he said he relies on audience engagement to produce a collective acknowledgment of the everyday intricacies of race and racism in the lives of Black Americans.[7] In his view, they also demand a level of emotional vulnerability, so he uses his corporeal body and emotive life as the sites of this community building. Chappelle's remarks demonstrate how vulnerable his comedic process is, and they make clear that his vulnerability inadvertently set the terms for the premature end of his wildly successful television show. Chappelle tells Angelou, "With laughter when I'm at my best I'm not looking for it. But you kind of get sensitive about how people laugh. When I left my show it was because I did this sketch ["The Nigger Pixie"] and I knew what I intended but somebody laughs differently than I intended—and I caught it. It was painful."

Chappelle's embrace of emotional vulnerability reflects his role as a post-soul satirist. Coined by Nelson George, the term "post-soul" points to the contemporary moment in which Black cultural producers, especially satirists, attain a discursive space in which they may subvert, challenge, and laugh about representations of Black Americans.[8] They have been afforded this space by the repeal of de jure segregation, the unprecedented socioeconomic advancement of a small subset of African Americans, and widespread popular claims of a postracial cultural political sphere. Mark Anthony Neal asserts that is the potential of the post-soul aesthetic to radically reimagine "the contemporary African American experience, attempting to liberate contemporary interpretations of that experience from sensibilities that were formalized and institutionalized during earlier social paradigms."[9] A post-soul aesthetic fits well with the kind of satirical freedoms that *Chappelle's Show* was celebrated for, such as the popular sketch "Frontline," featuring Clayton Bigsby, played by Chappelle. Bigsby is a blind orphan whose upbringing in the rural South has given him the unique ability to become the leader of a white supremacist group. In an introduction to the sketch, Chappelle stated, "I showed it to a black friend of mine and he looked at me like I had set black people back with a comedy sketch ... sorry."[10] In previous generations, Black vanguards suppressed stereotypical images and racial epithets about Black people. There is a well-documented history of the National Association for the Advancement of Colored People and its periodical *The Crisis* leading numerous crusades to stop the circulation of D. W. Griffith's *The Birth of a Nation* (1915), *Amos 'n' Andy* (1928–1960), and other sites

of popular culture that circulated harmful stereotypes and caricatures of Black people.[11] If W.E.B. Du Bois asserted that "all art is
propaganda and ever must be," then Chappelle mentioning that
he "had set black people back" suggests that his use of stereotypes
could be misinterpreted or be more harmful for Black people
than good.[12] They likely would have frowned on the sketch's
copious use of the N-word and racist stereotypes. But as the audience's laughter confirms, post-soul can depart from sanctimo-
nious images of racial uplift and shift toward irreverence about
racially sensitive material.

For Black visual satirists, the concept of laughter is complicated. On the one hand, they hope the audience's laughter
acknowledges both the ironies and absurdities of living as a person of color in a country that proclaims freedom and democracy. Such laughter of resistance recognizes the fortitude of these
people as they negotiate the ever-evolving American racial landscape. On the other hand, white supremacist sensibilities may
invade a space intended for communal catharsis, thus leaving a
satirist vulnerable to misunderstanding and to a barbed, racist
laughter that reifies hegemonic power and racist ideologies. Satire
is a multivalent, duplicitous form that laces acerbic wit with
digestible amounts of laughter, and it is aimed at audiences who
approach the material with varying levels of cultural, historical,
and political knowledge. Such entanglements produce layered
laughter, the by-product of a collective meaning-making process
wherein multiple sites of laughter create multiple meanings. While
some comedians attempt to corral these meanings in longer satires, the brevity of sketch comedy limits performers' ability to
frame their message. Chappelle's solution was to introduce his
prerecorded sketches in front of a live viewing audience, an
attempt to mediate viewers' laughter and their meaning-making
process.

As psychoanalysts, sociologists, and humorists have noted,
societal rules and norms mediate the physical and psychological

process of laughing. "Only jokes that have a purpose," Sigmund Freud wrote, "run the risk of meeting with people who do not want to listen to them."[13] The interplay of intent and reception is key in post-soul exchanges of laughter. In *Laughter and Ridicule*, Michael Billig asserts, "Some acts of humor might appear rebellious to the participants, those who laugh might imagine that they are daringly challenging the status quo or transgressing stuffy codes of behavior. . . . However, the consequences of such humour might be conformist rather than radical, disciplinary not rebellious."[14] In other words, as Rebecca Krefting clarifies, "even if stereotypes are introduced as cultural myth we cannot say with certainty that viewers will not misinterpret performances to fulfill rather than challenge existing beliefs, to reinforce rather than raze stereotypes."[15] For Freud, Billig, and Krefting, the intent of laugher does not always translate into the right kind of laughter. While the intrinsic ambivalence of post-soul laughter is supposed to jettison any discrepancies between a cultural producer's intent and his or her reception, the peculiarity of minstrelsy as a performance tradition has complicated this process for Chappelle. The urge that postmodern Black satirists have to represent scenes of bondage acknowledges the impact of slavery on conceptions of blackness and the impossibility of a realistic representation of slavery in the contemporary moment.

Conventional scholarship on humor is overwhelmingly concerned with the audience's perception and consumption of the humor and thus tends to undervalue what Ralph Ellison called "the sheer joy of the joke." According to him, "The Negro's 'masking' is often motivated not so much by fear as by a profound rejection of the image created to usurp his identity. Sometimes it is for the sheer joy of the joke; sometimes to challenge those who presume across the psychological distance created by race manners, to know his identity. Nonetheless, it is in the American grain."[16] Ellison redirects our attention to the pleasure of producing this type of humor. Chappelle's joy is the

2.1. The *Chappelle's Show* stage during the pilot episode.

catharsis he experiences when he laughs and makes others laugh. By centering his satirical voice and perspective on race, he demonstrates his self-care as he joyfully makes sense of the world around him—a move that complicates historical narratives of White consumptive laughter of Black funny men. Chappelle demonstrates that alongside, and in spite of, this reductive laughter, Black joy in the form of unapologetically centering oneself is "the sheer joy of the joke."

Central to Chappelle's vulnerability on stage is a performed apathy about his reception—that even as he unapologetically prioritizes his Black interiority and comedic sensibilities there is a performance of ambivalence toward his audience and their laughter. Chappelle's studio stage is the primary site of his comedic catharsis; it re-creates the stand-up stage and allows him both to be physically close to his audience and to perform the desired response for that audience (Figure 2.1). His singular stage presence foregrounds his physiognomy and laughter, allowing them to serve as a hermeneutic for interpreting the psychology of his unique style of satire. In the DVD audio commentary for season 1, Chappelle and his longtime writing partner and friend Neal Brennan discuss the stage and the improvisation that the comedian uses to connect with the audience. As Chappelle explains, his stand-up roots helped him foster a relationship with his audience, so he has difficulty focusing on the camera. Thus, in *Chappelle's Show*, the stage privileges his laughter over the audience's; in contrast to the approach in other sites of racially charged humor, the camera rarely pans to the laughing audience to show their tacit acceptance of the joke. There are a few memorable moments in which Chappelle laughs within the narrative scope of a sketch—for instance, at the end of "The Niggar Family," when he says, "This racism is killing me inside."[17] Unlike the vulnerable laughter he shares with the audience on the stage, Chappelle's diegetic laughter in "The Niggar Family" sketch has more of a sobering effect than a cathartic one. According to Danielle Morgan this moment is "meant to destabilize the mainstream acceptance of and propagation of the racial status quo and do so surreptitiously by feigning carelessness."[18] Dave Chappelle's laughter during this sketch as well as others falls outside the realm of catharsis because Dave Chappelle has not prepared the audience for the critique or laughed with them. Mutuality is key if the performance is to function as a potential occasion for redress.

In conversation with Angelou, Chappelle mentions a moment when a White crewmember "laugh[ed] differently than I intended, and I caught it."[19] This person's "particularly loud and long" laughter did not register as solidarity, and Chappelle's recognition of this difference may allow us to reshape popular interpretations of his abrupt departure.[20] Articles and interviews in *Time* and *Newsweek* suggest that drugs, partying, and mental health contributed to his decision to stop the show and also indicate the influence of misunderstandings and racial paranoia. However, Chappelle's "I caught it" remark illustrates his ability to exert power over laughter that is meant to diminish him. He walked away from the show as an agent who knew the possibilities and limitations of his cultural impact.

Pixie Problems

"The Nigger Pixie" sketch begins with Dave Chappelle sitting in a first-class airplane seat as a White flight attendant approaches him. She greets him as "Mr. Chappelle" and asks whether he wants chicken or fish for his meal.[21] Chappelle is the only person of color in the sketch and the only one who is visibly uncomfortable. As he listens to the flight attendant, a pixie appears on the back of the seat in front of him. This pixie is a technologically altered miniature of Chappelle in blackface acting in the traditional minstrel role, speaking broken English and using exaggerated bodily gestures. The figure is a racially stereotyped, visual representation of the comedian's subconscious. The pixie says to Chappelle, "I just heard the magic word, chicken. Go on ahead and order you a big bucket, nigger, and take a bite . . . Black motherfucker." Then it begins to tap dance (Figure 2.2). Chappelle wants the chicken, as his inner pixie demonstrates, but worries about how Whites around him will interpret his blackness if he succumbs to the stereotype. He irritably says to the flight attendant, "I'll have the fish thank you very much." The repartee becomes more hostile when the frustrated pixie says, "You son of a bitch, you don't want no fish." The sketch succeeds in trivializing the decision, especially after the pixie taunts, "Maybe it's catfish."[22] At the same time, it successfully demonstrates that there are both internal and external stakes in how one publicly performs blackness in the post–civil rights era.

Throughout the sketch, Chappelle remains preoccupied with verbally one-upping the pixie. His investment in winning grows as he rehearses different ways to eat the fish. The pixie is the object against which he can gauge his own "progress," and their repartee demonstrates his ambivalent attachment to an idea of

2.2. Dave Chappelle in blackface for "The Nigger Pixie" sketch during episode 2, season 3, of *Chappelle's Show*.

blackness that has been forged through a history of dehumanization, the production of a robust, attendant discourse, and the cultivation of community, culture, and positive self-identification. Furthermore, although the pixie is an antagonistic entity bent on dehumanizing him, it also represents Chappelle's internal strife. It personifies his anxieties about belonging in the predominantly White, affluent space of first class. He needs to dominate these anxieties, yet the pixie's catfish taunt demonstrates the impossibility of achieving a subjectivity that is wholly detached from stereotype. At the end of the sketch, Chappelle finally gets up from his seat to escape the harassment. Yet there is nowhere else to go on a plane; and because the pixie is embedded in his subconscious, it would follow him regardless. The sketch is a visual reminder of the legacy of slavery and the way in which it envelops the mundane moments of Black life, even something as trivial as choosing an inflight meal.[23]

In the initial airing, the segment included Chappelle's friend, the rapper Yassin Bey, then known as Mos Def. He was a pixie sidekick, playing banjo music so that Chappelle's blackface pixie could dance minstrel-show jigs. But both the online and DVD versions remove Bey from the sketch, and Comedy Central changed key details to mitigate any backlash from Bey's caricature. For instance, it has archived the sketch on its website as "The Stereotype Pixie" rather than "The Nigger Pixie."[24]

A brief clip follows "The Nigger Pixie" in which Chappelle's Black pixie comments on the Ying Yang Twins' *MTV Cribs* episode.[25] "I never thought I'd say this, but I'm embarrassed," the pixie says, commenting on a scene in which the rap duo pick up a wooden monkey statue and perform an emphatic monkey call. Now the pixie is no longer manifesting Chappelle's racial anxiety but gauging whether Black cultural production advances stereotypical images of blackness. The segment illustrates Chappelle's perception that certain Black artists are enacting something worse than minstrelsy—unabashed Black buffoonery. It also legitimizes the pixie's cultural authority from the perspective of respectability politics because his embarrassment represents a cultural logic that disavows such buffoonery.

The two sketches reveal Chappelle's cognitive dissonance about issues of Black authenticity and authority. On the one hand, he demonstrates his commitment to representing nuanced Black life by disrupting monolithic notions of blackness and Black masculinity with sketches such as "When Keeping It Real Goes Wrong," in which Black men and women are portrayed as uncool and physically and emotionally vulnerable to racial ideologies of blackness. On the other, as the second "Nigger Pixie" sketch shows, his relationship to neo-soul and hip-hop points to his belief in the cultural, political, and moral grounding of blackness.

Pixies appear in other sketches in the same episode of *Chappelle's Show*, illustrating the pernicious effect that stereotypes have on all Americans. A Latino pixie tempts a Latino man

(Guillermo Diaz) to buy stolen automotive seat covers, and an Asian pixie tries to convince an Asian man (Yoshio Mita) to mispronounce television personality Lala Anthony's name. Two sketches feature White pixies, whom Donnell Rawlings introduces by exclaiming, "This is for all the crackers that ain't here." In these sketches, Chappelle, in his popular whiteface, tempts a White man to not dance with Latinas and not to look down when standing at a urinal next to a Black man.

At the end of the episode, Rawlings and Charlie Murphy explain in a prerecorded segment that Chappelle left the show because of "The Nigger Pixie" sketches. As evidence, they highlight excerpts from his interview with *Time* and conclude, "At the taping, he wondered if the new season of his show had gone from sending up stereotypes to reinforcing them."[26] The highlighted quotations do not include the comedian's complaint that "one spectator, a white man, laughed particularly loud and long" and Chappelle's admission that "it made me uncomfortable." Instead, the text intimates that his reservations about the direction of the show were unwarranted. The voiceover declares that Comedy Central is invested in creating a guilt-free laughing experience, unmediated by questions of propriety and racial guilt, for all audiences. It notes that the network's neoliberal investment in an amoral racial humor is supposed to evoke a narrative of racial progress. Yet the segment also demonstrates the psychic hold of slavery on both Chappelle and a large part of his viewership. As a close-up of Rawlings replaces the image of the *Time* article, he says, "We didn't know if we should air the sketch or not, so we asked the audience." In other words, would re-creating the types of conversations about race that the show was famous for assuage the tension of airing episodes that Chappelle had said he did not want to air?

The subsequent conversation with the audience sees most of those interviewed expressing their love for the show and downplaying the charged humor in the episode. Yet one audience member says, "I feel like [the pixies are] derogatory to black and Spanish people but [play] on the good stereotypes of white people." Another states, "I thought the sketch was cool. The only problem is ... the white race is seen as the generic race." Both dissenting audience members are Black, and both imply that there is no comparable situation in which a White racial performance will produce a similar level of anxiety and stereotypical imagery. Their comments reinforce the potentially offensive nature of the episode and clarify why Chappelle might have had reservations about letting his audience view it. During the conversation with the audience, Rawlings and Murphy frequently return to the racial diversity of the pixies to legitimize the episode's production and airing. They also keep mentioning the White pixie to mitigate issues of representation.

MINSTREL MUSINGS

Because of its appropriation of Black emotionality during slavery, minstrelsy has enduring racist iconography that is frequently mined for Black satire. Eric Lott asserts, "While [minstrelsy] was organized around the quite explicit 'borrowing' of black cultural materials for white dissemination, a borrowing that ultimately depended on the material relations of slavery, the minstrel show obscured these relations by pretending that slavery was amusing, right, and natural."[27] Similarly, Michael Rogin states, "Democratized from the court and the plantation, minstrelsy enacted the urban white desire to acquire African American expressive power and supposed emotional freedom without actually freeing the slaves."[28]

Minstrelsy, which dates back to the mid-nineteenth century, grew out of a White working-class vaudeville tradition.[29] Initially, White working-class actors would blacken their faces with burnt cork and dance and sing for White audiences throughout the North and the South. The productions popularized stock caricatures of Black Americans as lethargic, simpleminded, and

happily subservient, and set the standard for their later representation in theater, television, and film. Thomas Rice's "Jumping
Jim Crow" minstrel routine became so associated with Black life
and culture that the moniker was used to name the Jim Crow
laws, the codes that enforced southern segregation and inequality
well into the mid-twentieth century.

According to Daphne Brooks, pre–Civil War White minstrelsy was praised for its skill and attention to detail, but by the
late nineteenth century most members of the public believed
that the Black minstrels who stepped into this premade entertainment were better able to tap into the Black American experience.[30] Thus, the minstrel is the first widely acknowledged
artificial racial representation that has ironically produced a narrative of authenticity. This ironic legacy set the terms for Chappelle's "The Nigger Pixie" and the type of laughter he hoped to
receive, even as he playfully referred to himself as "a real live
coon" to a *Newsweek* reporter on set.[31] His pixie represents the
extent to which racial stereotypes are dialectically illogical and
artificial yet derived from actual desires and characteristics. Furthermore, it emphasizes the greater stakes for this contradiction
as it ensnares people of color.

The cultural labor of White laughter in the minstrel tradition,
"in which blackface comic and white spectator shared jokes about
an absent third party, usually resolved to a configuration of two
people, the joker personifying the person being joked about." The
suggestion was that this simplemindedness produced an unintentional buffoon, who, when juxtaposed with the ideals of White
masculinity, created a sense of innate backwardness, thus producing
comedy. At the peak of minstrelsy's popularity, its cultural logic was
a repressive communal laughter that maintained racial markers of
whiteness and blackness as the concepts of freedom and enslavement shifted. Thus, the "racist pleasure" embedded in the visual
consumption of blackface "was converted through laughter and
humor into a beloved and reassuring fetish."[32]

Chappelle grappled with this legacy when he heard someone laugh longer and louder than he expected during the taping of "The Nigger Pixie." But what kind of laughter did he intend to provoke? Viewers of the prerecorded show hear laughter from the studio audience after examples of minstrel-like humor. Chappelle's intent was to represent the anxiety all people feel when stereotypes and lived experiences intersect; as Charlie Murphy asks in the intro, "Have you ever been in a situation where you feel racially insecure?" Murphy is referring to the moment in which racial ideologies converge on an individual's existential will. In Chappelle's multiple pixie sketches, these convergences range from the dismissive White man who does not follow his White pixie's dancing advice to the temporary madness of Black and Latino men whose pixies force them to try to escape. Yet the audience's laughter suggests that Chappelle's performance as a blackface minstrel is the defining characteristic of the sketch. Audience members laugh when the pixie's behavior is at its most racist.

Nonetheless, Chappelle's emphasis on racial insecurity and anxiety shifts the original joking formula of the minstrel stage. Originally, performers were able to create laughter from what Lott describes as the "oscillation between currency and counterfeit" or the interplay of authenticity and artificiality—a kind of reductive and often fictitious mimetic humor that invited audiences into the Black experience.[33] However, the interior nature of Chappelle's pixie, coupled with its direct hostility toward Chappelle, created a markedly different type of comedic engagement. As Chappelle's pixie argues with a Black man who is not in blackface, the sketch captures the tension between artifice and authenticity in a Black modern moment.

The pixie wears a porter costume that subtly conjures a legacy of Black labor and mobility. This legacy is particularly fraught in the first-class section of an airplane, where the terms of servitude have shifted: Chappelle is the passenger, and a White woman is the flight attendant. The symbolic class markings of the Black porter remind us that Black men's relationship to transportation is tied to a history of labor and lack of access. Like Aunt Jemima, the Black chef on the Cream of Wheat box, and the Black lawn jockey figurine, the notion of a Black porter carrying luggage through a train triggers a national nostalgia.[34] On the minstrel stage and in early cinema, performers purposefully evoked this nostalgia by wearing porters' costumes. In fact, in 1831, the aforementioned Thomas Rice borrowed one from a Black man named Cuff to wear when he performed an early version of his Jim Crow routine.[35] Chappelle's use of the porter iconography juxtaposes that history with the dynamic of sitting in the first-class section of the airplane. The pairing suggests that if a comedic redress is going to be successful, it has to be coupled with images of financial success.

To that end, *Chappelle's Show* couples other images of slavery with financial success. In "Time Haters: Great Misses," for instance, a group of player haters assembled in a previous episode exhibits the clothes and dispositions of stereotypical pimps. The sketch's concept is borrowed from the Players' Ball, an annual gathering of pimps. Here, the characters travel back in time to "hate," or play the dozens with people. In one outtake, they travel back to antebellum America so that the leader of the group, Silky (played by Chappelle), can call a slave owner a cracker. The sketch ends with Silky shooting the slave owner dead. In his remarks after the sketch, Chappelle says, "Apparently shooting a slave master isn't funny to anybody but me and Neal. If I could, I'd do it every episode."[36] Writing about this scene, Glenda Carpio argues:

> The fantasy of retribution finds violent, although also symbolic, outlet while the object of that violence is not, as in Pryor's scene of introjection, the black body. Yet the redirection to the white body of the master depends on simplified notions of retribution (and race) in which the crimes of

slavery, enormous as they are, would find some kind of redress in the shooting of a white man. Still, the fact that the skit provides cathartic release—both in the form of the light humor that precedes the violence act and the violent act itself—is important given the need for the redress of slavery when if only symbolically, that Pryor's, as well Rock's and Chappelle's, work make clear.[37]

The player haters' ostentatious fashion sense creates a narrative of financial success that is imbricated in Chappelle's meaning-making process of redress and catharsis. As Buc Nasty (Charlie Murphy) states, "You better watch your mouth, white boy, before I put these gators up your ass and show your insides some style."[38] Furthermore, because the sketch is presented as a flawed outtake, the act of screening it for an audience is itself a defiance in which the comedian privileges himself in these comedic moments to exchange a meaning-making process with his audience.

Like the porter costume, the centrality of chicken in "The Nigger Pixie" evokes a specific image—in this case, the Zip Coon stereotype and the cultural logic of disempowering Black masculine aspirations. In *Building Houses Out of Chicken Legs*, Psyche Williams-Forson writes, "The images of African American men, portrayed in the likeness of Zip Coon in compromising positions with chicken, are perverse and overwhelming."[39] She demonstrates that in the dominant popular culture of the late nineteenth century such images helped to inscribe Black people, particularly Black men, with an animalistic quality. This move, like many of the other caricatures of Black people in post–Civil War America, was intended to undermine their new-found citizenship. From Ralph Ellison's yam-eating Invisible Man to Chappelle's chicken-eating pixie, the inclusion of food in creative scenes has been a way to represent Black Americans' negotiation of "how power can be present in even the most mundane objects of our material lives."[40] Again, the enduring threat of dehumanization helps to create the racial anxiety that Chappelle captures in the sketch.

"The Nigger Pixie" echoes a bit in Chappelle's stand-up show *Killin' Them Softly* (2000), in which he recalls doing a show in Mississippi and afterward going to a restaurant where the White server tells him that he wants chicken. When Chappelle asks how the server knows what he wants, the server replies, "It is no secret down here that blacks and chickens are quite fond of one another." Chappelle responds, "I'm genetically predisposed to liking chicken. I've got no say in the matter ... [but] now I'm scared to eat it in public."[41] As the server's assumption and rationale demonstrate, the stereotype continues to animalize Black people. Thus, the minstrel complexities that Chappelle evokes create a palimpsest of meanings for his audience's layered laughter.

Chappelle is optimistic about creating a collective laughter and meaning-making practice that acknowledges and celebrates Black subjectivity. Yet he left *Chappelle's Show* in the middle of taping the episode that includes "The Nigger Pixie," thus forfeiting his 50-million-dollar contract. For contemporary African American satirists, the impasse of the current moment is a continued preoccupation with the power appropriated to race. Although we are living in the post–civil rights era, we are not living in a postracial era; and Chappelle's unraveling both inside and outside the sketch marks how he and other satirists have been unable to move past this conclusion. The pixie is a supernatural being beyond the plane passenger's control, and Chappelle's decision to use it as a character has given him a way to creatively articulate the forced suturing of Black people's psychic selves to a derisively stereotyped history of racial injury.

Chappelle's appropriation of blackface minstrelsy also manifests his personal turmoil. The passenger's phantasmagoric engagement with the pixie bespeaks an inner competing consciousness and contributed to the comedian's "clumsy dismount" from *Chappelle's Show*. Chappelle later said, "It had a little psychological element to it. I have trust issues, things like that. I saw some stuff in myself that I just didn't dig." Neal Brennan elaborated on Chappelle's psychological state: "He would come with an idea, or I would come with an idea, pitch it to him, and he'd say that's funny. And from there we'd write it. He'd love it, say 'I can't wait to do it.' We'd shoot it, and then at some point he'd start saying, 'This sketch is racist, and I don't want this on the air.' . . . There was this confusing contradictory thing: he was calling his own writing racist."[42] Chappelle's reactions suggest that something about the television frame was divorcing the final product from his original meaning. Perhaps, during the conceptualization phase, he had imagined an audience poised to participate in a cathartic response, but he later adopted a dominant gaze when producing and viewing the sketch. Indeed, as the crewmember's unexpected laughter affirmed, there is a disconnect between Chappelle's intent and the visual reception of his work. Whereas "white people, white artists, are allowed to be individuals," he declares, this is a "dilemma" for Black cultural producers, who have to be more critical about the images they create for popular consumption and the lasting effects they have on Black Americans.[43] Robert Patterson drives home this point when he writes, "The assumed realness of negative and stereotypical representations of black subjects and black life has had real (that is, meaningful, substantive, and material) consequences for black people and thus contextualizes why representation has been an important force for the making of black cultural politics."[44]

In the DVD audio commentary for the episode, Brennan, Rawlings, and Murphy reveal both their collective fatigue and their deep, lingering confusion about the sketch and its aftermath. Brennan says, "Being responsible was never a concern of the show until . . . it gets popular, then it's like, I guess."[45] As the three try to contextualize the audience members' problems with the White pixie, Brennan eventually states, "It didn't make a difference that we had two white pixies and we peed on them because it still doesn't undo all the awful shit white people have done in the history of the world." Murphy adds, "But that's not what the sketch was about," and Brennan replies, "The sketch stopped being what the sketch was about a long time ago."[46]

SUBVERTING THE MARKETPLACE VALUE OF SATIRE

During an interview with James Lipton, Chappelle said, "When art and corporate interest meet just prepare to have your heart broken."[47] His comment suggests that misplaced laughter was not his only reason for leaving *Chappelle's Show*. Rather, he realized that Comedy Central was economizing racial progress through his racial humor and the show's television ratings, co-opting his message and causing him to doubt his ability to make subversive critiques of large power structures. When designing the show, Chappelle had assumed that Americans would not be willing to take "a tour through a young black man's subconscious" and the show would be canceled quickly.[48] Throughout much of the first season, he noted on air that the show had not been canceled yet, perhaps referring tacitly to the short run of *The Richard Pryor Show* (1977). At the same time, he intentionally distanced his show from *The Chris Rock Show*—notably, with a fifteen-second clip during the pilot that announces, "It's not HBO. It's just regular-ass TV."[49] This early posturing shifted at the end of the second season, when was engaged in contract negotiations. He understood how power breathes life into structural forms of racism, and this prompted him to be more self-reflexive about the show's politics or its lack thereof: "Fifty million dollars is a lot of money," Chappelle said. "And what I'm learning is I am surprised at what I would do for $50 million. I am surprised at what people around me would do for me to have $50 million."[50]

Chappelle's awareness of his economic value to the network was stressful for the comic and frustrated his ability to make his art. For instance, when Comedy Central featured him on a panel discussion of the N-word, he knew the goal was to market his brand to position him as an expert on the subject. Although Brennan asserts, "There is no one from the network sitting on his head. Dave is in charge of his own world," Chappelle often felt otherwise.[51] In a 2006 interview with Oprah Winfrey, he said, "When you're a guy that generates money, people have a vested interest in controlling you. And I feel like the people that were trying to control me were putting me through stressful situations."[52] When addressing hints that drug use and insanity had influenced his premature departure from the show, he said, "Maybe corporate America fucks with human beings like they're products and investments."[53] His word choice evokes the long history of capitalism's exploitation of Black labor and happiness. This shift in language, from the nineteenth-century's *property* to the twenty-first century's *product and investment*, substantiates the expansion of capital in Black cultural production and links Black cultural producers to what Houston Baker refers to as the economics of slavery and Blacks' ability to appraise themselves in this economic landscape.[54] As Chappelle's father told him early in his career, "Name your price before you get there. And if you ever find it's more expensive than what you're prepared to give, then get out."[55]

The logo of Pilot Boy Productions, Dave Chappelle's production company that aired at the end of every episode of *Chappelle's Show*, illustrates the tensions among financial success, neoliberalism, and an attempt at redress and catharsis. The image shows a shirtless, shackled Chappelle holding handfuls of money. In the accompanying voiceover, Rawlings shouts, "I'm rich, bitch!" The voiceover is from "Reparations 2003," a sketch that in Carpio's words pushes the stereotypical "carrying out [of] white fantasies about race to their most absurd levels."[56] Chappelle's depiction as both enslaved and rich reifies his position to the network. His expression is cautious; his face is slightly tiled away from the camera, his eyes glance sideways, and his pursed lips are solemn. Rawlings's voiceover creates figurative reparations for viewers, but Chappelle's static image suggests that this reparation comes at a cost to himself. He does not look happy.

Although Chappelle resisted network television's commodification of him as a race man, his departure from *Chappelle's Show* and subsequent return to the spotlight embodies the slippages around the race man in this contemporary moment. There is a compulsory element to the race man and our collective infatuation with designating Black men to this role. Chappelle's return to the spotlight was difficult for the comedian. He had a few stand-up routines in 2014 that ended with him being heckled on stage and poorly reviewed.[57] In 2016, however, he signed a major deal with Netflix for 60 million dollars to release three comedy specials. The Netflix deal addresses two major concerns in re-creating the terms for people's compulsory desire to see Chappelle as a race man. First, it eliminated the role of the network and in doing so afforded Chappelle a level of autonomy that worked with his views on celebrity and artistry. Second, for communities that had felt that Chappelle was being true to his authentic self and to his blackness in how he left his television sketch comedy show, the Netflix deal presumably replaced the Comedy Central deal that Chappelle walked away from. It is also important to note that this deal was for stand-up routines and not a sketch comedy show. Stand-up routines are confined to a specific moment in time and often location in ways that differ from the constant production of a sketch comedy show.

Nevertheless, as Chappelle's fame grew his unique, off-brand humor increasingly moved away from annunciating the complexity and levity of Black life to using homophobic and transphobic jokes to critique political correctness. If we agree with Bambi Haggins that in the early 2000s Dave Chappelle was the provocateur in the promised land, then by 2017 that promised land was newly equipped with the social awareness of strides in

LGBTQIA+ communities and the #MeToo movement and was less enamored with Chappelle's approach and content.[58] The shift in Chappelle's content and reception is in part the product of the changing landscape of the country. Chappelle's humor is couched in a Generation X sensibility that is probably better defined by its ambivalence and popular culture than by its sociopolitical movements. However, with the changing social, cultural, and political landscape during Trump's presidency, Chappelle's approach did not have the same resonance with Millennials and Generation Z and their unflinching stance on social awareness. We can also read his fight against political correctness as an unwavering defense of his famous friends, colleagues, and profession. Comedians were at the center of a number of scandals around the #MeToo movement and queer communities. Bill Cosby, Louis C.K., and Kevin Hart were all either legally or culturally called into question, and Chappelle defended them not with the same nuance he uses to think about the precarity of blackness but with jokes that situated disenfranchised groups as responsible for their own undoing. For instance, in *Sticks and Stones* (2019), after he defiantly claims that he is what is known as a victim blamer and goes on to say that when he was told that Chris Brown hit Rihanna his initial response was "What did she do?"[59] Within this logic, Chappelle's own beleaguered proximity to celebrity that I outlined above is the culprit behind his and other comedians' issue with "cancel culture."

In the third series of *My Next Guest Needs No Introduction*, David Letterman speaks to this desire when he asks if Dave Chappelle considers himself a leader. Chappelle responds that he does not consider himself to be a leader and nor does he want to be one. Letterman acknowledges that he is turning to Chappelle to provide insightful commentary after incidents involving race and racism, states, "I'm waiting for you to say something. What does that make me—a follower?"[60] Letterman was referring to

Chappelle's 2020 Netflix special *8:46*, a stark Black Lives Matter performance titled after the length of time law enforcement officer Derek Chauvin kneeled on George Floyd's neck before he died. Letterman's question breathes life into the nexus of the funny man and the race man and the way that Chappelle has woven together aspects of both. During the routine, Chappelle criticizes Don Lemon's call for Black celebrities to make a statement about the recent deaths that were used as a part of the Black Lives Matter movement in the summer of 2020. Chappelle notes that "this is the streets talking for themselves, they don't need me right now."[61]

Chappelle starts *8:46* by thanking the young protesters leading the Black Lives Matter movement and connecting Floyd's death to the deaths of John Crawford III, Michael Brown, and Trayvon Martin. On the one hand, this is a classic Chappelle complaint. He continues to be frustrated by the way that his celebrity propels him to speak on issues around race and racism. On the other hand, Chappelle recognizes why he is sought after for this social commentary when he states during his performance that, "You don't expect me to be perfect. But I don't lie to you. I'm just a guy . . . and every institution that we trust lies to us."[62] Chappelle situates himself as a truth-telling griot, similar to his poetic understanding of Kendrick Lamar's 2018 performance at the Grammys that opened this book. It is Chappelle's supposed authenticity that makes him an apt race man. However, he shows the limitations of the race man in the twenty-first century when he continues to create a genealogy of Black death that leaves out the names of Black women who have died at the hands of the police. Breonna Taylor's death was highly publicized during the summer of 2020, and Chappelle's failure to incorporate her story in this performance demonstrates how his embrace of the race man figure continues to exist at the expense of Black women and queer communities. While the image of George Floyd's death and his pleading for his mother in his final moments captivated the world, it was the persistent vulnerability and erasure of Black women in conversations about state-sanctioned violence and feelings of loss and failed potential for Black women that were being acknowledged in the attention paid to Breonna Taylor's murder and the hashtag campaign #SayHerName.[63] Chappelle's performance attempted to represent the inner emotional life of Black people, but his failure to include Black women demonstrates that his worldview is limited to Black men.

Chappelle's performance is also notable for the ways he is announcing that others are leading the way through the Black Lives Matter movement and that he no longer is the person that best articulates Black life in this moment, even as he attempts to wrestle with and perform a Black masculine anguish and rage for America. In many ways, Chappelle's acknowledgment that others are better suited to lead this moment reveals the nature of the dynamic between contemporary race men and actual forms of protest and social activism. The Black Lives Matter movement has not made a concerted effort to utilize Black celebrity like the civil rights movement did in attracting prominent celebrities like Harry Belafonte, Sidney Poitier, and James Baldwin to expand the reach of the protests and the movement as a whole. That is not to say that Black celebrities are not taking part in the Black Lives Matter movement. Indeed, there have been prominent images and videos of rappers, professional athletes, and actors present at marches and rallies. However, the movement hasn't been interested in spotlighting that type of celebrity.

Ultimately, Chappelle recognizes that the trope of the race man is a concept that he embraces at strategic moments when he is being a storyteller of Black history, creating and focusing on archives of Black men involved in masculine pursuits, whereas he avoids the trope of the race man when he uses humor to critique celebrity culture and his frustration with political correctness. As Danielle Morgan asserts, "In this way, Chappelle's later comedy has suffered from his lack of vulnerability and his association with—and newly discovered comfort among—those in positions of power."[64] Fortunately, Chappelle does not attempt to speak with the full weight of blackness when he uses shock comedy to talk about celebrity culture or political correctness. With the emergence of the Black Lives Matter movement and the political stakes for Black leadership rising, Dave Chappelle seems to be more self-aware about his limitations and the limitations of the funny race man.

CHAPTER 3

Integrationist Intimacies

IN CHAPTERS 1 AND 2, I extended the concept of vulnerability from a discourse of trauma and precarity to the inner emotional lives of Black men. I first argued that part of the twenty-first-century retreat from the allure of the race man is through the embrace of a sociopolitical form of nihilism that liberates a unique intersection of race and gender for Black men that instead allows them to turn inward. I then highlighted the ways that Dave Chappelle, a visual Black satirist, was susceptible to neoliberal articulations of race work and humor and what that meant for the interiority and emotionally vulnerable process of sharing his humorous outlook with the world. I want to take this chapter to reconsider what happens when vulnerability is both a site of trauma and self-reflection for Black men. As Kevin Quashie asserts, "Conceptually victimization and vulnerability are nearly synonymous, hence both are judged to be antithetical to the nationalist cause.... Rather than being seen as a quality of an inner life and a necessary human capacity, vulnerability comes defined as a liability to black survival."[1] Quashie's words remind us that, historically, the rejection of vulnerability and its conflation with victimhood even in the face of injury was a complicated emotional display of strength. This performance of strength for Black men was foundational to Black nationalist discourses and their investment in cultivating and maintaining public collectivism—albeit a collectivism that centered Black men at the erasure of Black women and Black queer folks. Although Quashie's work brilliantly parses the distinctions of vulnerability and victimhood to argue that vulnerability is necessary to attend to the inner lives of Black folks, what happens when victimhood is present? What shifts in the public and private lives of Black men when they need to attend to their violation? Does it preclude them from race work? What is generative about a vulnerability steeped in violability?

This chapter takes up Percival Everett's satirical novel *I Am Not Sidney Poitier* (2009) to center the relationship between sexual violation and Black boyhood and show the similarities and differences between the desires projected onto Black boys' bodies during Barack Obama's presidency and the civil rights movement. By examining Everett's novel, in particular the early scenes of sexual abuse suffered by the adolescent narrator, this chapter argues that sexual violation annunciates the multiple ways Black boys and men's bodies are vulnerable to White liberal consumption in postracial America.[2] Within contemporary satire, satirists represent rape as what I argue are moments of narrative rupture and emotionlessness. This affectless space is a clear departure for narrators in satirical novels who generally possess a unique mastery of describing the absurdities of sociocultural, historical, and political convergences in the mundane lives of the people around them. The protagonist's voice in contemporary satirical novels is cerebral and meticulous for its rigorous stream of consciousness that often levels numerous critiques in a sentence. However, depictions of sexual violence depart from that condensed, arrhythmic musing to render rape and its afterlives as distinctly outside of the broader multivalent, postmodern aesthetic, and instead attend to the emotional labor and sociocultural work of victims and survivors. The departure from the narrative voice in *I Am Not Sidney Poitier* constitutes Black boys as rapeable subjects by demanding that the reader sit with and through the protagonist's sexual violation. If rape and sexual abuse are understood as some of the most direct and pernicious ways power gets enacted on the body, then representing Black boys as uniquely vulnerable to these corporeal intrusions highlights a continuum of Black masculine sexual vulnerability while arguing that violated but living Black masculine bodies are still in need of help.

BLACK MEN, SEXUAL STEREOTYPES, AND VIOLATIONS

White supremacist heteropatriarchy tethered Black men's sexuality to the Mandingo and Black Buck stereotypes. The Mandingo stereotype, named after the Mandinka people of present-day Sierra Leone, is the long-held belief that Black men have larger penises and are more virile. Stereotypes about Black men's sexuality date back to the transatlantic slave trade as a way of alluding to the reproductive possibilities of Black bodies on plantation and still inform numerous assumptions about Black men's bodies across the diaspora. The legacy of these stereotypes is present in the trend of White women traveling as sex tourists to West Africa and the Caribbean to have sex-filled vacations with Black male sex workers who are often referred to as bumsters, rastitutes, and beach boys, and it is also present in interracial cuckolding, wherein Black men are the preferred "bulls" or "studs." While gender and race complicate these sites of neocolonial sexual desire in ways that differ from more well-established forms of sex tourism—specifically White men traveling to Asia, these sexual economies are largely predicated on the sustained belief that Black men are better sexual partners.

In the United States, the Mandingo stereotype runs parallel to the Black Buck caricature. Michel Foucault maintained that "power is essentially what dictates its law to sex. Which means first of all that sex is placed by power in a binary system: licit and illicit, permitted and forbidden."[3] The history of slavery and the racist stereotypes that continue to define Black men's bodies as

deviant, criminal, and hypersexual complicate the relationship
between power and sex for Black men's sexuality.

White supremacists created the myth of Black men's insatiable sexual appetite during the postbellum era. The stereotype
dominated America's imagination and helped legitimize the
racialize violence and terror of groups like the Ku Klux Klan.
The central conceit of the myth of the Black Buck within this
white supremacist framework of surveillance and violence is
that without the constant policing that the institution of slavery
provided, Black men would revert back to their natural inclina-
tions of violence and sexual aggression. Institutions of power
that serviced White men's interests insisted that without their
proper supervision Black men would attack White women and
threaten whiteness as a whole, a belief that has proved useful in
the dissemination of racist ideology. During slavery, slave masters
denied Black men's sexuality any positive social significance
other than to exploit it as a means of increasing their property.
Almost forty years after the end of Reconstruction, the success
of D. W. Griffith's 1915 film *The Birth of a Nation* would in part
act out the continued national fascination and fear of Black sexuality, with one of the more iconic moments in the film featuring a man in blackface threatening to rape a White woman.
Of this moment, Michael Kimmel suggests that "the new and
powerful fear of the black rapist revealed more about southern
white men's fears of lost manhood than about any propensity on
the part of black men."[4]

With lynchings becoming a popular form of vigilante "justice," this anxiety resulted in White men manipulating the law,
and "castration quickly became a part of the summary hanging
prescribed for black males accused of sexual offenses."[5] As Trudier Harris, Koritha Mitchell, and others have asserted in their
articulations of the staged ritualistic violence of lynchings, sexual offenses oftentimes served as lies fabricated to induce fear in
Black communities by ripping Black men from successful Black

businesses and families.[6] Sandy Alexandre cogently traces this property dispossession and theft back to Ida B. Wells when she states that "while conflict over property—construed materially as land, as house, or as store—often underlay the ritual lynching of blacks, it was the lynchers' claims to White southern woman-hood that repeatedly served as lynching's ritualistic pretext."[7] I would extend Alexandre's analysis by arguing that the lynchers' focus on the sexual lives and "purity" of White women was bound to a fear of, and fascination with, Black men's sexuality.

Due to the peculiar institution of American slavery, the proximity of African American sexuality to power has always been a complicated one. In *The History of Sexuality: An Introduction*, Foucault suggests that when addressing the role and impor-tance of sexuality, "the objective is to analyze a certain form of knowledge regarding sex, not in terms of repression or law, but in terms of power."[8] For Foucault, power is defined by who has control over the status of illicit and licit sexuality. In other words, who is able to sanction sexuality and what are the by-products and politics at play in sanctioning it. Outlining the origins of this complicated history, Patricia Hill Collins in *Black Sexual Politics* explains the way that Black bodies were reduced to laboring parts. For Black men, this meant that their sexuality was made illicit through the ways that they were deemed bestial or, as Collins suggests, some hybrid between man and animal that lacked the elevated thought to be considered wholly human. As part of their assumed closeness to animals, the mythos around Black men's sexuality dictated that they were innately violent and hypersexual in ways that their slave masters ostensibly needed to constantly police. Collins writes, "Taming the beast in order to produce the buck involved domesticating Black men's predilection for violence, placing their brute strength in service to productive manual labor, and directing their natural albeit deviant sexuality toward appropriate female partners." She goes on to say, "In this fashion, White elites reduced Black men to their bodies, and identified their muscles and their penises as their most important sites."[9]

The historical and contemporary preoccupation with Black men's penises—originally articulated as a sign of their subhuman status—is the product of purposeful attempts to make a spectacle of Black men's anatomy; something to which Black men's subjectivity and claims of power can be reduced to. The historical staging of blackness has confined Black sexuality to the pornographic and bound Black men's subjectivity to the physical. This preoccupation with the pornographic in many ways echoes Audre Lorde's problem with the prevailing definition of the erotic, where she argues that "in order to perpetuate itself, every oppression must corrupt or distort those various sources of power within the culture of the oppressed that can provide energy for change. For women, this has meant a suppression of the erotic as a considered source of power and information within our lives."[10] For Lorde, patriarchal frameworks' conflation of eroticism and pornography creates a sight of erasure around a source of energy and a sense of completion that robs women of their full potential. Black men's sexuality initially was defined in terms similar to Lorde's articulation of the erotic and the ways that it has been co-opted and perverted by heteropatriarchal societies.

Historically, the trope of the race man has played out its own sexual fantasies and desires. As Hazel Carby outlines, W.E.B. Du Bois replaced sexual desire with work ethic and intellectualism, but to suggest that all race men or would-be race men displace sexual desires in favor of more intellectual or spiritual pursuits would limit the way we think about Black men's sexuality and sidestep difficult conversations about the power dynamics of Black men leveraging their power to seduce Black women.[11] In this #MeToo moment, it is important to acknowledge the role that the figure of the race man plays in the trope of the philandering, and sometimes sexually coercive, Black preacher and/or politician.

Sexing the Race Man

In order to better understand Percival Everett's character "Not Sidney Poitier" and his attempt to negotiate the White liberal consumption of his body, we must first turn to the actual Sidney Poitier and the civil rights movement to see how the desire for the race man plays out in White liberal fantasies. In August 2009, President Barack Obama awarded Sidney Poitier the Medal of Freedom, the highest award given to a civilian, at the White House. Although there were a number of prominent and influential people being awarded that day, such as Stephen Hawking, Sandra Day O'Connor, Billie Jean King, and others, there was an undeniable connection between the film icon of the civil rights movement and his political, prodigal son making good on the sit-ins, boycotts, onscreen interracial kisses, and desegregated classrooms. Sidney Poitier's seminal representation of the often-successful integrated Other is a popular culture predecessor for Barack Obama and the space he inhabits in the American imagination.[12] Both men are a part of a Black cosmopolitan class that troubles their proximity to the institution of slavery in the United States, thereby situating them as the exotic (Black) Other. Ultimately, Poitier created a nascent example of Black respectability on the silver screen that Obama later personified in his political career. Mia Mask and Ian Strachan see the relationship between Obama and Poitier differently: "What people saw in candidate and President Obama, they had seen decades before in the Poitier persona: cool, eloquence, genuine warmth, exceptionality, and ambiguity of identity. It was clear . . . Poitier had primed the white American imagination . . . for the historic election of the first black President of the United States."[13]

The identity and characteristic traits that Poitier and Obama share are emphasized through a shared investment in their bodies and their physical attractiveness—an attractiveness that often made and continues to make their social, cultural, and political work more palatable to predominantly White liberal audiences. Take, for example, Amber Lee Ettinger's viral video/song "Crush on Obama," and the cadre of articles that took up the president's attractiveness.[14] In 2014, the *Washington Post* asked "How Attractive Is Barack Obama?"[15] A month later the *Huffington Post* answered with the article "Why You Find President Obama Attractive."[16] White liberalism, in turn, masks Whites' fetishization of these nouveau-raced and yet postracial men as a mark of racial progress. They function as the sexually seductive side of racial progress. Poitier, like Obama, is the model of a respectable Black masculinity that is always clean-shaven and dressed in slacks and a button up.[17] In the previous chapter, I examined how contemporary satire uses nihilism to divorce Black men from the trope of the race man, and in this chapter, I extend that analysis to give space to examine the relationship between Black boyhood and sexual violence as it relates to the race man. In short, this chapter annunciates the broader sexual vulnerability of Black boys and the ways that White liberalism consumes their bodies as a necessary site of race work. White liberalism routinely fantasizes the intimacy of integration and fetishizes Black boys and men's bodies as would-be race men that force sexual encounters that recreate racist power dynamics. The issue of consent and sexual violation stands in as one of the many ways to show that narratives of Black.

Similar to the cultural fixation on Obama's attractiveness, the film industry centered tacit articulations of Poitier as a site of taboo desire that created an integrationist gaze on the silver screen. This gaze relied on Poitier's characters being in close proximity to White actresses, via either an intimate form of touch or an endearing look. The integrationist logic and work of Poitier often takes shape along gendered lines for the White characters he shared the screen with. White male characters are often the site of hostile, racist White conservatism, such as Chief Gillespie in *In the Heat of the Night* (1967) and Tony Curtis in *The Defiant Ones* (1958), while White women were often situated as the more liberal voice of reason and open to change and racial progress.[18] It was at these two poles of whiteness where Poitier's body was consumed for racial progress, and it was often this "erotic life of racism" and the seduction of integration that began these transformations with White women en route to White masculinity.[19]

Born in Miami, Florida, and raised in the Bahamas, Poitier was the youngest of seven children. He is arguably the most iconic actor of the civil rights movement. His body of work routinely situates him as the lone Black voice in predominantly White spaces that are forced to grapple with the quotidian reality of integration. In the twelve years between *Brown v. Board of Education* in 1954 and Martin Luther King Jr. assassination in 1968, often considered the time frame of the civil rights movement, Poitier was in twenty-six films. In addition to *In the Heat of the Night* and *The Defiant Ones*, films like *Blackboard Jungle* (1955), *Lilies of the Field* (1963), *To Sir with Love* (1967), and *Guess Who's Coming to Dinner* (1967) all leave Poitier's character negotiating antagonistic, White worlds that he is tasked with either saving or changing.[20] Within this body of film, I am particularly interested in the films where Poitier primarily shares the screen with White women and where White men are absent.

Within the matrix of Black culture and public life of the civil rights movement, Poitier's body of work, and quite literally his corporeal body within that work, was a persistent site of tenuous race relations. His body of work is deeply situated within the iconography of the civil rights movement, an iconography that Nicole Fleetwood suggests "loves the black subject whose struggles for equality represent the possibilities of

American democracy."[21] Unfortunately, what has always been possible in American democracy is sexual exploitation and consumption. For instance, in *Lilies of the Field* Poitier shares the screen almost exclusively with a small group of White women—specifically East German nuns. The film is about Homer Smith, a Black itinerant worker who stops at a remote and deteriorating home in the desert for water and to attend to his overheating car. After taking on several small jobs for the nuns that he is never paid for, Homer inadvertently stays at the house to help build a church for the nuns. The integrationist gaze creates a tacitly understood sexual tension between Homer and the nuns. Although the nuns are represented as pious and celibate, Homer is represented as a secular entity in the house that is changing some of the cultural norms. Moreover, the trailer for *the film* focuses on Mother Maria, the head nun, and her early assertion that God would send her a "big strong man." A narrator reiterates Mother Maria's assertion and then leaves space for sexual possibility, "a big strong man—just what five lonely women were looking for."[22] Like all Poitier films, the sexual politics and possibilities in *Lilies of the Field* always lie just under the surface. Rarely are nuns described as being lonely, so to include this language in the trailer for the film creates sexual innuendo where none exists. Although one could argue that the film is not one of Poitier's more civil rights–oriented films, it does represent how race and racism impact issues of religion, labor, and entrepreneurship. It is important to note that while the film does demonstrate a broader understanding of race with its setting in the U.S. southwest and its centering of a local Hispanic community, it is Homer's forced free labor that he wants to be paid for that drives much of the plot in the film. The film operates as a larger narrative of Black determination and self-reliance as Homer is able to build a church with little resources, which ultimately leaves him with a sense of accomplishment and purpose. In this way, the film seems like an adaptation of the biblical story of Noah's Ark, one infused with American racial politics to suggest that Black people have the capacity to build but lack the direction to realize their potential.

Poitier's star power among Black audiences was always two-fold. Sharon Willis argues that what she terms "the Poitier effect" is "symptomatic of enduring fantasies that shape popular white-authored representations of race. It represents a dream of achieving racial reconciliation and equality without any substantive change to the 'white' world or to 'white' culture, and especially, to white privilege."[23] On the one hand, Poitier personified a version of Black respectability and commitment toward equality that prompted Martin Luther King Jr. in 1967 to state, "He is a man of great depth, a man of great social concern, a man who is dedicated to human rights and freedom." On the other hand, that same year of 1967 Clifford Mason asked the provocative question "Why Does White America Love Sidney Poitier So?" in the *New York Times*.[24] The answer for Mason and others was that Poitier failed to represent a version of blackness that had fully actualized a positive image of Black people. Yes, Poitier helped move the film industry from using unapologetic racial stereotype and caricature to a more nuanced representation of blackness. But such "gradualism" has limitations for Mason: "It may have some value in politics. But in art it just represents a stale, hackneyed period, to be forgotten as soon as we can get on to the real work at hand."[25] Mason goes on to contend that "until the concern of movies is for the dignity, the manhood, the thinking of the Negro in his world, with its historical past, its turbulent present and its hopeful future, there can be no true portrait of the Negro and no true art."[26] In short, Mason sees Poitier consistently being situated in White spaces and fixing White problems as the crux of the problem of Poitier's ability to extend Black representation on the silver screen.

Willis states that the Poitier effect is "a compensatory gesture, averting or deflecting the possibility of a kind of critical thinking that would involve a serious reciprocal interracial exchange, instead offering a fantasy of racial understanding and 'assimilation' that requires no effort on the part of white people."[27] If we agree with Willis that Sidney Poitier signifies "a handy trope for imagining conciliatory interracial encounters," then we must also reckon with how White directors and audiences rendered Poitier's dark, athletic body as an illicit site of desire to play with what Sharron Holland refers to as the "erotic life of racism."

In *To Sir, with Love* Sidney Poitier plays the role of Mark Thackeray, an out-of-work engineer who is forced to take a position as a teacher in an inner-city school in the rough East End of London.[28] The film inverts the well-worn White savior trope where a White person triumphantly goes into the inner city to teach students of color about their subject area and their humanity. In addition to inverting the racial dynamics of this Hollywood trope, the film also sees Poitier come full circle: his breakout role was as a student in the film *Blackboard Jungle*, where he plays a delinquent who, with the help of his White teacher (Glenn Ford) is able to become a beckon of hope and respectability for his predominantly White classmates.

In *To Sir, with Love*, Poitier's Thackeray teaches White people how to be racially inclusive and morally grounded. Nevertheless, Poitier's body and sex life are routinely centered in the film. The opening scene shows Thackeray riding a bus through the streets of London in between two White women. The scene is meant to show the lower socioeconomic space Thackeray will be teaching and at the same time, through his close proximity to these White women, to demonstrate the stark contrast from the U.S. context in which he usually finds himself on-screen. In fact, Poitier's sitting between these two White women evokes the image of Rosa Parks sitting on the Montgomery Bus discussed in chapter 1. The two women begin a conversation about cooking dinner that quickly turns sexual. The woman sitting next to Thackeray says, "I wouldn't mind having this little lot in my stocking for Christmas, eh." She gestures toward Thackeray, and the woman she's speaking to retorts, "Ah you wouldn't know what to do with it, you've been a widow too long." The scene ends with all three people laughing as the bus drives along. These women talk around and through Poitier's body. He never says anything. The scene marks a kind of brazenness that often gets attributed to lower socioeconomic statuses, but Poitier's body in the scene ensures that it is also read along racial lines. Whiteness does not worry about respectability politics toward Black people or its reduction of Black bodies to flesh.[29] Although the age of these White women leaves them outside of the scope of Thackeray's work of making a decent White populace, the scene illuminates the way that Poitier's body is vulnerable to White women's sexual desires and the ways that those desires are supposed to mark an integrated postracial landscape.

Although Hollywood used Poitier's presumed sexlessness as a way to consistently position him as the safe, respectable image of blackness, as *To Sir, with Love* demonstrates, is the promise and potential of sex that informs Poitier's ability to reach White women in his films. However, as I have described above, Poitier's characters are never the ones that advance this promise and potential for sex, and that holds true for *To Sir, with Love*. Later in the film, one of Thackeray's students, Pamela Dare (Judy Geeson), becomes attracted to him (Figure 3.1). As she begins to embody the life lessons of respectability and class that Thackeray is imparting in his classroom, it is through her attraction to her teacher that she becomes aware of her classmates' racism toward him. Thackeray never reciprocates the student's affection, but it is her affection that begins to shift the racial politics of the film.

SEX AND THE (UN)CIVIL RIGHTS MOVEMENT

The history of sexual violence animates Black violability. As scholars have shown, this is especially true for Black

3.1. Mark Thackeray (Sidney Poitier) talking to Pamela Dare (Judy Geeson) in *To Sir, with Love* (1967).

womanhood across social, political, and cultural spaces. Since slavery, Black men's and women's bodies have been understood as sites of wanton libidinal desire that helped to promulgate the myth that Black sexuality was insatiable and deviant. The southern plantation economy used these myths to help morally ground Black people's legal designation as property and therefore, as Saidiya Hartman asserts, their inability to be raped. According to Hartman, "The rape of Black women existed as an unspoken but normative condition fully within the purview of everyday sexual practices, whether within the implied arrangements of the slave enclave or within the plantation household."[30] As Jim Crow segregation replaced slavery and the culture of dissemblance organized around respectability politics, Black people, primarily Black women, created separate sexual lives from their social lives.[31] Fanny Lou Hamer asserted during the civil rights movement that "a black woman's body was never hers alone," and scholars like Darlene Clark Hine and Hartman recentered racist narratives about rape from Black men and White women to the lived experiences of Black women and White men to tend to the gaps in the literature and to make space for realities like Hamer's.[32] If we agree with Aliyyah Abdur-Rahman that "representations of sexual perversity under conditions of enslavement have contributed to notions of sexual alterity and to the ideologies by which aberrant sexual practices were named, domesticated, and policed," then our understanding of sexual violence and vulnerability is heavily mediated by the institution of slavery and its suturing of violence and sexuality.[33]

As Thomas A. Foster asserts in his centering of Black masculine sexual violence in the economy of the antebellum South, just as Black women lacked the basic claim to humanity needed for sexual consent, the sexual violation of Black men took various forms that also foreclosed sexual consent.[34] Within the African American literary canon, scholars like Maurice Wallace and Darieck Scott have outlined the ways that Black writers represent sexual trauma for Black men and the impossibility of consent, specifically in Toni Morrison's *Beloved* (1987) with Paul D on the chain gang, and in Frederick Douglass's *The Narrative of the Life of Frederick Douglass* (1845), with his witnessing the whipping of Aunt Hester.[35] These scholars' attention to nineteenth-century iterations of sexual violence serves as an important intervention or fleshing out of the body of scholarship on rape and blackness. What I wish to emphasize is that Black men's relationship to sexuality, like that of Black women, was born out of an institution of exploitation and theft and highlights slavery's ability to commodify and confine Black bodies.

By the 1950s, the racialized violence of the Jim Crow South was being increasingly hidden from the public eye. During the height of Jim Crow, southern Whites routinely enacted mundane public expressions of racial superiority through discrimination, segregation, and racial and sexual violence. The days of lynching advertisements and postcards with mutilated flesh were replaced with covert forms of racialized violence. The use of television as a tool to propagate the injustices of the Jim Crow South meant that civil rights movement was dichotomized into public and private spaces—private acts of violence were brought into the public space.

The fear of Black sexuality guided white supremacists' responses to the litany of civil rights activists and organizations flooding the South during the late 1950s and 1960s. Throughout the South, white supremacists routinely centered stereotypes about Black men's licentious sexual desires in their machinations to condemn civil rights activists traveling into their small rural communities. As Danielle L. McGuire writes, "As Northern volunteers flooded into [Mississippi] in June 1964, white Mississippians braced themselves for what they considered a military—and sexual—invasion."[36] Similarly, historian John Dittmer suggests that White Mississippians "made interracial sex a centerpiece of their attack on the summer project."[37] The fearmongering about Black men's sexuality conjured the basest desires of white supremacy—a kind of Freudian obsession with Black sexuality, a fascination that James Baldwin interrogates in his short story "Going to Meet the Man."[38] Such fearmongering also obfuscated the centrality of sexual assault as a mechanism of white supremacy.

NOT THEIR RACE MAN

Percival Everett's *I Am Not Sidney Poitier* is a coming-of-age story about "Not Sidney," a young Black man that shares an uncanny resemblance to Sidney Poitier. Although there is a rumor that Poitier may be his father, there is not a direct lineage tied to the civil rights actor.[39] Throughout the novel Everett weaves together the plots of different Poitier films such as *The Defiant Ones*, *A Patch of Blue* (1965), *In the Heat of the Night*, and others to evoke a civil rights logic and sensibility that Not Sidney routinely departs from in order to demonstrate the fragility and absurdity of Poitier's integrationist iconography and how this contemporary post–civil rights moment will no longer engage in the same racial overtures toward White people. For instance, when in *The Defiant Ones* two prison fugitives Noah Cullen (Sidney Poitier) and John Jackson (Tony

Curtis) attempt to catch a train in order to get away from the authorities, Noah jumps off the train after he realizes John is too slow to catch it in act of racial solidarity or, as James Baldwin argues, to reassure "white people, to make them know that they're not hated."[40] Baldwin states, "When Sidney jumps off the train, the white liberal people downtown were much relieved and joyful. But when Black people saw him jump off the train, they yelled, 'Get back on the train, you fool!'" In Everett's novel, Not Sidney finds himself similarly running from police officers after he is arrested for "being Black" but fails to wake his associates, stating, "The train's whistle blew. It was coming and I was the only one awake. I did not wake them. The locomotive passed, and I walked to the tracks. Just as Sis had said, the train was moving very slowly up the grade. I found an empty boxcar and easily climbed into it. Alone. I left them sleeping there where they belonged, with one another."[41] The slowness of the train and Not Sidney's decision to not wake his companions demonstrates the break in representation from *The Defiant Ones* to Everett's novel. If we agree with Baldwin that Poitier's original scene comforts White America and lets them know that Black America does not hate them, then Everett's twenty-first-century postscript suggests that Black America is no longer burdened with such acts masked as solidarity.

Everett's picaresque novel follows Not Sidney's cross-country adventure from his miraculous birth in Los Angeles to a financially savvy, quirky mother whose untimely death sends an eleven-year-old Not Sidney to live with media mogul, Ted Turner, one of his mother's early investment beneficiaries, in his Atlanta mansion. Not Sidney goes to school in Atlanta and later attends Morehouse College. The novel ends with Not Sidney leaving college and heading west to see what's on his mother's headstone. Not Sidney's episodic tale echoes Everett's earlier novel *Erasure* (2001) for the ways it highlights the absurdities of American racial politics. Negation is a central construct in post–civil rights aesthetics and Black cultural production. With any

periodization marked by "post-," boundaries are drawn and maintained based off of stark distinctions of a new sociocultural
moment in relationship to the one that preceded it.

Vulnerable Black Boys

After arriving in Atlanta to live with Ted Turner, Not Sidney
begins high school. Shortly after, his White history teacher, Miss
Hancock, sexually assaults him. Although Not Sidney states that
"an inappropriate and, I must say, welcomed relationship began
to surface," the protagonist echoes the societal sentiment that
pubescent boys always welcome sexual advances and that they
cannot be adversely affected by early sexual activity with a person in power like their female counterparts can be. After accompanying his teacher to her house to help her with gardening
supplies only to open the truck upon arriving and see nothing
but "a spare tire, a jack, and jar of petroleum jelly," Not Sidney is
asked, "Do you know what fellatio is?"[42] It is in this moment that
the reader is able to attach meaning to the subtle humor of Miss
Hancock's name as a portmanteau of hand and cock. Not Sidney
narrates the rape in the following way: "In her house, and I'm not
certain how she got me in there, the teacher put her mouth on
my penis and sucked on it." The simplicity of Not Sidney's narration about his sexual molestation is not in keeping with the rest of
the narrative, and although he states a page earlier that the relationship was welcomed, his inability to be self-reflexive about the
moment demonstrates a clear break from the narrative voice
throughout the novel. Furthermore, the narrative tool of trans-
temporal and spatial dreams that remove him from the scene to
happier moments that accompany his violation departs from the
prevailing narrative style that is overwhelmingly consumed with
being mentally and emotionally in the present moment. Everett's
choice to move toward fragmentation and abstraction in an otherwise cerebral text is in keeping with other satirists and their narration of Black boys being victims of sexual violence.[43]

The early scene of sexual violence comes to define the subsequent moments of sexuality in the novel, making the issue of
consent central to this coming-of-age novel and the distinction
that Everett draws between the civil rights movement and post–
civil rights moment. Throughout the novel, oral sex serves as
both a violent and pleasurable act that always creates nostalgia
for Not Sidney. During his early molestation, Not Sidney states,
"My eyes rolled back into my head, and I recalled the long,
drawn-out, luxurious days of my youth. . . . I was enjoying the
memory . . . when sharp pain brought me back."[44] The sharp
pain that Not Sidney is referring to is Miss Hancock's teeth biting during the oral sex. Not Sidney's victimization and the
shared space of pain and pleasure that he inhabits during his
assault evokes Ursa's act of empowerment at the end of Gayl
Jones's *Corregidora* (1975).[45]

Corregidora is a first-person, stream-of-consciousness narrative about a blues singer, Ursa, who is dealing with a miscarriage
and hysterectomy at the hands of her abusive husband, and the
cyclical intergenerational trauma of slavery and its legacies of
violence and sexual objectification for the women in her family.
Ursa recognizes that history violently converges with the present moment and that her family's history of sexual violation
haunts her current pain. In order to psychically process her
emotions, she has to exorcize her foremothers' pain and desire
toward their Brazilian enslaver, Corregidora. At the end of the
novel, Ursa is back with her estranged husband about to perform fellatio on him as she contemplates what her great grandmother did to Corregidora in order to (re)claim her agency.
Ursa thinks, "What is it a woman can do to a man that make
him hate her so bad he wont [*sic*] to kill her one minute and
keep thinking about her and can't get her out of his mind the
next? . . . A moment of pleasure and excruciating pain at the
same time . . . a moment that stops before it breaks the skin."[46]
Ursa realizes in the moment of sexual intimacy that the threat of

castration and violence through an intentionally sadistic performance of fellatio is how she can conjure her past to free her
future. According to Ashraf Rushdy, "What Ursa's interpretation
of the family secret . . . teaches her and allows her to reveal to us
how both Great Gram's and Ursa's acts are historically resonant
and part of a collective endeavor of redefining the role of sexuality and desire in acts of resistance and of producing desire out
of resistant activity."[47] Ursa's sadistic fellatio is a resistant act to
reclaim her agency in spite of the backdrop of enslavement
and lynching wherein Black men's castration and consumption
was ritualized. Great Gram tells Ursa the story of a woman on a
neighboring plantation who cut off her master's penis instead of
submitting to her sexual violation. In retaliation, "[slave owners]
cut off her husband's penis and stuffed it in her mouth, and then
they hanged her. They let him bleed to death. They made her
watch and then they hanged her."[48] Great Gram with this story
of castration conveys to Ursa the stakes for Black women resisting sexual domination.

While historically Black men and women's ability to resist
sexual domination has taken different forms, the stakes are
always death. When Not Sidney asks what happens if he does
not submit to Miss Hancock's desires, she states, "If you leave,
then I will fail you and you'll never graduate from high school
and you'll never get into college and you'll waste away on the
street until you turn to drugs and die hopeless, helpless, and
alone."[49] Miss Hancock subscribes to respectability politics and
the notion that education can help substantiate one's existence
in an anti-Black world, so if she is able to compromise Not Sidney's education then she has successfully compromised his
means for survival, thereby sentencing him to death—the same
fate as the woman in Great Gram's story. In Not Sidney's
encounter with Miss Hancock the roles are reversed and he,
unlike Ursa, is not grappling with how to assert his sexual
agency and subjecthood. Instead, Not Sidney is trying to figure

out how to reclaim his body from a White woman in a place of authority who imagines herself sexually satisfying him yet is okay with physically hurting him during sexual assault. While performing fellatio suggests a type of sexual submissiveness, it is the coercive nature of the engagement and Miss Hancock's "practice until we get it right" that constitute different racial entanglements for Not Sidney and Miss Hancock, which are nevertheless on the same axiological space of sexual domination as Ursa's historical reclamation. If we agree with Rushdy that Ursa's decision to embody her great grandmother's experience with her enslaver with her estranged husband puts the type of violence that she endures in conversation with the horrors of slavery, then Miss Hancock's physical threat of castration and emasculation engages a history of lynching wherein White patriarchy imbued White women with the power over Black men's lives.

Not Sidney radically acknowledges his own victimhood when he states, "Without the chewing and chomping, the fellatio became pleasurable in that animal way that any kind of genital manipulation is pleasurable to a teenage boy, in spite of her name being Beatrice, in spite of the audience of dinner bells, in spite of my being a victim."[50] Not Sidney's ability to recognize his own victimhood is important for the way that it announces to the reader precisely how he is not Sidney Poitier and is unwilling to let his body be the fodder of White liberal desire.

Prior to Not Sidney's second episode of sexual abuse at the hands of Miss Hancock, Everett uses the connection between Not Sidney and Sidney Poitier to convey the historical and cultural significance of Not Sidney's sexual abuse. The second time Not Sidney is in Miss Hancock's house, he takes note of her extensive bell collection, especially one that Miss Hancock says she got from Sparta, Mississippi, at a hotel called the Tibbs Inn, evoking *In the Heat of the Night*. The reference to the film is important because it is one of the looser references to Poitier's corpus in the novel and is followed by Miss Hancock saying that the hotel sells Tibbs Ribs. *In the Heat of the Night* is about a Philadelphia detective, Virgil Tibbs (Sidney Poitier), who is wrongly accused of murder in the small town of Sparta, Mississippi. Tibbs has to help the racist local police department solve the murder in order to be vindicated. Miss Hancock's mentioning of the barbeque dish seems tangential, but when considered with the long history of lynching and consumption in the creation and maintenance of White women's sexual and moral purity, it illuminates the historical stakes and intergenerational power of White women in scenes of sexual economies with Black men. The history of lynching included the common practice of mutilating corpses for souvenirs, White consumption, and burning Black bodies, all of which were routinely performed as a way to uphold and protect White womanhood, and it is that history that Miss Hancock is able to synthesize in her mention of Tibbs Ribs.

Vincent Woodard reminds us that other more metaphorical and sexual forms of consumption "took on more intimate, erotic connotations within the domestic sphere of the plantation, where social death rather than literal death was the preferred outcome."[51] Additionally, the use of Tibbs in this manner minimizes arguably the most important quote from the film. When Sheriff Gillespie is ridiculing Virgil about his name by stating, "That's a funny name for a nigger boy that comes from Philadelphia! What do they call you up there?" A frustrated Tibbs replies, "They call me Mr. Tibbs!"[52] Virgil's radical declaration of "They call me Mr. Tibbs!" is a reminder of his personhood, and his emphasis on "Mr." attends to the infantilization of Black men in the South who were routinely referred to as boys throughout their adult lives. The histories of infantilized Black men and the legacy of lynching violently converge in the name Tibbs Ribs, and is a reminder of the stakes of resisting Miss Hancock. While Everett does not suggest that Not Sidney is aware of the historical significance of Tibbs Ribs, it is important to note that he does demonstrate an awareness toward the mundane absurdities of race and racism and the role that the civil rights movement had in creating these realities. It is at this moment in the novel that Miss Hancock realizes the full weight of her position as predator and the power she is able to enforce over Not Sidney's body as both his teacher and a White woman. "Go ahead, report me," she says. "Who will they believe? Me, teacher of the year, or you, a kid without a proper name, angry because he couldn't live out his fantasy with the hot teacher."[53] Miss Hancock's thinly racialized discourse demonstrates both the way in which Not Sidney, as Black object, is not able to inhabit the role of the victim because of his "anger" and improper name, and the way in which she, as hot (White) teacher, is not understood within our sexual and racial lexicon as predatory.

Not Sidney's narrative voice during and after his scenes of abuse reflects the mental, emotional, and psychical stakes of Black boys' susceptibility to acts of sexual violence. When he tries to report his teacher to the principal, he states, "I found myself unsure about how to proceed with my accusation. I could not say blowjob to the principal and neither could I say to him that Beatrice Hancock had given me head or fellated me, so I landed, like a blind roofer, on rape. 'She raped me,' I said, regretting it before I had uttered the final word."[54] Not Sidney's wit is beginning to return in his ability to process his sexual violation, his "so I landed, like a blind roofer, on rape." The ineffability of his trauma is both reflective of a broader inability of sexual assault survivors to name their accusers, but is also mediated through the assemblage of his gender and racial identities. As a Black boy whose body is mediated through images and assumptions of sexual dominance and physicality, Not Sidney is outside of the cultural logic of the sexual assault victim, and the regret that Not Sidney has for articulating his trauma as "rape" demonstrates the discursive limitations in being able to claim a kind of innocence and purity that is aligned with being vulnerable to sexual violence that has historically been denied to blackness. The principal's response to Not Sidney's admission should have been one of profound sincerity. Instead, Not Sidney recalls, "I never heard such laughter. Mr. Clapper turned beet red, his tongue rolled into a tube and pushed out of the O of his mouth as he coughed, and tears trickled down his corpulent face while he pointed at me. I think he said, *that's rich*, or maybe, *you wish*, or *that bitch*, which made no sense. But it was clear, clearer than clear, that he did not believe me."[55]

Not Sidney's moment with the principal's office demonstrates the power dynamics for sexual assault victims coming forward to name their attackers. Rape and other forms of sexual assault and violation are endemic to exercises of power. As Rebecca Wanzo asserts, "Discourses about rape are often a vessel for other issues, and scholarship about rape typically addresses the ways in which rape is an act that reveals something about the workings of power, property, sex, violence, and pain."[56] The lack of humor for the reader and the on-page laughter of White hegemony shifts the terms of LaMonda Horton-Stallings's articulation of BDSM satire and the way she locates how Black masculine masochism subverts dominant articulations of Black masculine gender formations. After the violent response of laughter from what should have been Not Sidney's support system, Not Sidney makes a radical decision about his future:

> I decided right then to light out for the territory, as it were, to leave my childhood, to abandon what had become my home, my safety, and to discover myself. . . . And so, this became a prophetically, apocalyptically instructive, even sibylline, moment. I was, in life, to be a gambler, a risk taker, a swashbuckler, a knight. I accepted, then and there, my place in this world. I was a fighter of windmills, I was a chaser of whales. I was Not Sidney Poitier.[57]

What was "apocalyptically instructive" for Not Sidney is that assumptions about race and gender would continue to inform White people's assumptions about his body and sexuality. However, he radically chooses to not be a conciliatory figure who is more concerned about the White people working through their investment in his physical body than he is about his own physical and mental well-being.

Not Sidney's ability to narrate his sexual violation and the solemnity that he uses to retell his abuse is a narrative rupture where humor's constitutive meaning making is avoided in service of highlighting the vulnerability of negotiating sexual trauma. Although the episodic nature of *I Am Not Sidney Poitier* suggests a type of ephemera surrounds the vignettes of Not Sidney's life, the protagonist's early rape scene informs the rest of the novel. Not Sidney's sexual violation and status as survivor in a novel that juxtaposes civil rights logics, aesthetics, and iconographies with the assumed "postracial" malaise during Obama's presidency represents the legacy and evolution of historical and political convergences that create white supremacist power structures—power structures that adversely affect Black people's psyche and relationship to their bodies, where no one is left untouched.

For the rest of the novel, Not Sidney's sexual health and bodily autonomy are shaped by this early violation and become a primary site of negation between him and Sidney Poitier. In this way, Everett centers an emphasis on consent for Not Sidney. Consent for Not Sidney is both literal and metaphorical. Not Sidney wants consent over his body as well as a metaphorical consent for how White liberalism and respectability politics takes up his body to create its own meaning and narratives. For Not Sidney, he continues to wrestle with the growing expectations around his body and time, and the way he is meant to placate White liberalism as he enters in and out of the narrative

landscapes of Sidney Poitier. Ultimately, the bodily autonomy of
Not Sidney allows the narrative to reveal the post–civil rights
assumptions and desires that White liberalism maps onto Black
men's bodies and sociopolitical platforms. Like his earlier novel
Erasure (2001), Everett ends *I Am Not Sidney Poitier* with a moment
that can be read as hysteria or madness. Not Sidney makes his way
west and arrives at an award show where everyone believes he is
Sidney Poitier. Although the novel ends with this conflation and
Not Sidney asserting that he does not feel like himself, the early
emphasis on sexual assault and its recurrence as a theme throughout the novel suggests that the negation is also around expectations written on and experienced by the body.

CHAPTER 4

The President and
His Translator

> But anger expressed and translated into action
> in the service of our vision and our future is a
> liberating and strengthening act of clarifica-
> tion, for it is in the painful process of this
> translation that we identify who are our allies
> with whom we have grave differences, and
> who are our genuine enemies.
>
> —Audre Lorde

IN CHAPTER 3, I examined the ways that Black
satirists negotiate White liberal consumption and desire on the
body of the race man via sexual trauma and assault. In this chapter, I explore the growing pressures of White liberalism to think
through how emotionality—specifically anger—gets incorpo-
rated into the neoliberal project of postracialism. Specifically,
I am interested in charting how the public demands for Barack
Obama's use of anger during his presidency were both a political
and social expectation of White America and the robust history of policing Black emotionality. I argue that White America
desired to co-opt Black men's political rage during Obama's
presidency and that the only space Obama felt that he could
subvert this demand was on the White House Correspondents'
Association (WHCA) annual dinner stage through the use of

comedians who would take up race, specifically his bringing the
Key and Peele (2012–2015) character Luther the Anger Translator
on to translate some of his remarks in 2015. I examine early
moments from Obama's presidential campaign and first term to
see how the public responded to his lack of emotionality—
specifically the public's call for the president to be angrier. I argue
that the WHCA dinner served as an important tool of the first
Black president. Obama epitomized the figure of the twenty-
first-century race man but was able to use the levity and wit of
the annual dinner to attack his political opponents, media outlets,
and broader American racial politics.

Historically, dominant culture has obscured sites and expressions of Black rage in order to dismiss the connection Audre
Lorde makes above between anger and action. Intentionally
obscuring anger becomes a way to marginalize and Other
someone by failing to recognize the source of their anger and
the underlying human experience behind their rage. For Black
people, the ability to publicly perform anger is almost always read
by dominant culture as illegible or illogical for the ways that it
relies on assumptions about Black criminality and deviance. This
is especially true for Black women who have to wrestle with having their tone, directness, and complexion constantly being mis-
characterized. There are real-world consequences of Black women
having to contend with the stereotype of the Sapphire, the attitu-
dinal, overbearing Black woman, and the first of these is the erasure of their anger. Black men's anger and rage is equally as
complicated because of their proximity to American heteropatriarchy and its reliance on anger and rage as a discursive tool.

bell hooks argues that "ultimately in imperialist white-
supremacist capitalist patriarchy Black male rage is acceptable,
expected even. No one really wants to hear Black men speak their
pain or offer them avenues of healing."[1] Indeed from Blaxploitation films to gangsta rap, Black men's rage is centered in popular
culture as an often commodified and co-opted way of reducing

Black masculinity to a singular affective terrain and performance. The embodiment of Black masculine rage in popular culture often gestures toward a "racial performance that [is] historically marked by notions around criminality, deviance, and pathology."[2] As such, prominent instantiations of Black masculine anger approximate the well-worn stereotype of the Black Buck, a physically dominant, violent, and sexually promiscuous figure that circulated as a central fiction during the Jim Crow era to animate racialized violence and obscure the racialized sexual violence that Black women were experiencing at the hands of White men. The figure of the Black Buck in our contemporary imagination sits at the nexus of race, class, and gender for the ways it misnames Black men's performances of anger. This misnaming is felt differently across the range of various socioeconomic classes, with dominant culture rendering poor Black men's anger the most obscure. Within the white supremacist, capitalist, heteropatriarchal structure hooks names above, dominant representations of Black masculine anger make a spectacle of Black rage in order to substantiate society's ease with the surveillance and policing of poor Black men while undermining the systemic reasons for their anger. Nevertheless, Black men routinely perform anger within this capitalist logic as an attempt to be legible in a broader American (read "White") masculinity, which as Michael Kimmel asserts has become increasingly angry in the twenty-first century.[3]

I argue that hooks's claim that Black male rage is acceptable flattens the reality and representation of many Black men and their nuanced performances and negotiations of anger. As William Grier and Price Cobbs assert in their seminal text, *Black Rage*, "Throughout his life, at each critical point of development the Black boy is told to hold back, to constrict, to subvert and camouflage his normal masculinity. Male assertiveness becomes a forbidden fruit, and if it is attained, it must be savored privately."[4] While I question Grier and Cobbs's use of "normal masculinity" and the broader ways they codify a narrative of emasculated Black boys and men, they do provide a nascent articulation of the various ways that Black masculine anger and rage are disparaged in the matrix of American heteropatriarchy. Similarly, Frantz Fanon states that "affect is exacerbated in the Negro, he is full of rage because he feels small, he suffers from an inadequacy in all human communication, and all these factors chain him with an unbearable insularity."[5] Despite his gendered language, Fanon maps a broader articulation of anger and rage and its "insular" expressions for the African diaspora, which in concert with Grier and Cobbs's gender-specific articulation of anger illuminates the private life of specific performances of Black masculine rage. How can Black men embrace public performances of anger that disavow heteropatriarchal articulations of American masculinity?

ALL THE RAGE

Historically, Black men have had a complex relationship to the production and expression of anger. I intentionally use the language of production and expression as a way to illuminate the psychological, emotional, and sociopolitical ramifications of Black men's public performances of anger. With my interest in production and expression I am not suggesting that anger has been completely foreclosed to Black men and women throughout history. Indeed, there were transgressive and subversive ways in which Black people across the diaspora felt, processed, and performed anger on and against their bodies. As Brittney Cooper reminds us "Americans love sassy Black women," but "owning anger is a dangerous thing."[6]

Within American heteropatriarchy, anger is thought to be the singular emotional space that men, primarily White men, have access to as a masculine emotional endeavor. According to Kimmel, "Angry white men are genuinely floundering—confused and often demoralized, they experience that wide range of emotions. But their anger is often constructed from those emotional materials, given shape and directed at targets that serve other interests."[7] What complicates our collective ability to recognize the various registers of White men's anger is whiteness's broader ability to obfuscate the various systemic manifestations of their anger and rage. As Carol Anderson asserts, "White rage carries an aura of respectability and has access to the courts, police, legislatures and governors, who cast its efforts as noble, though they are actually driven by the most ignoble motivations."[8] If we agree with Anderson and Kimmel that anger by way of fear comes to define contemporary White masculinity and that that anger has been normalized through its proximity to hegemony, then it is important to note that White masculinity rationalizes both this fear and anger as part of a logic of loss. The logic of loss suggests that as women, racial minorities, and LGBTIA+ groups achieve success in the road toward equality they diminish the privilege and power of White masculinity. In doing so, hegemonic forms of White masculinity cleave to nostalgia as a mental space to embrace the relational power of White heteropatriarchy. Black men engage in a similar logic of loss around the cultural specificity of slavery and colonialism.

Within some Black feminist texts, toxic forms of anger are racialized to the extent that when Black men take part in the abuses of patriarchy it is their close proximity to whiteness that prompts that abuse and anger. For instance, at the beginning of *We Real Cool: Black Men and Masculinity*, bell hooks asserts that "the gender politics of slavery and white-supremacist domination of free black men was the school where black men from different African tribes, with different languages and value systems, learned in the 'new world,' patriarchal masculinity."[9] While one could argue that the production and expression of anger was antithetical to the fight toward freedom and equality during slavery and Jim Crow, in a late twentieth century post–civil rights moment Black men used anger to demand political expediency and as an aesthetic for cultural production or the more

dangerous quotidian expressions of rage in their personal lives—
especially toward Black women and Black queer folks.

When Obama took office in 2009 news media outlets were
in awe at his unwavering professorial presentation.[10] Historically,
White supremacy has understood Blackness as a site of excess that
needs to be confined, dominated, and surveilled. While this excess
is primarily mapped onto the body, White supremacist frameworks also understand Black emotionality as excessive. Knowing
this history, the first Black president knew that he was going to be
held to a different standard. By 2009 the spectacle of Black masculine anger and rage in twenty-first-century mass media had
been classed, complexioned, and represented as violent and igno-
rant forms of self-destruction. The relationship between anger
and rage as the emotional underpinnings of revolution and Black
political thought was largely understood as extinct and laughable.
As Hortense Spillers writes in "Destiny's Child: Obama and Election '08," "The president understands that, as a black man . . . he
cannot, he dare not, show anger."[11] Within this logic, Obama's
inability to comport to White America's emotional needs made
the rise of Donald J. Trump inevitable.

THE PROFESSORIAL PRESIDENT

Early in the Obama era there were two nascent examples of
how Senator Obama and later President Obama would confront
issues of race and racism while tacitly evoking a narrative of
racial progress that undergirded his campaign slogans of "Hope"
and "Yes We Can." Sara Ahmed states, "Hope is crucial to the act
of protest: hope is what allows us to feel that what angers us is
not inevitable, even if transformation can sometimes feel impos-
sible. Indeed, anger without hope can lead to despair or a sense
of tiredness produced by the 'inevitability' of the repetition of
that which one is against."[12] Ahmed's attention to the dialectic
between hope and anger demonstrates that anger was a necessary
precursor to Obama's emphasis on hope during his presidential

campaign. Obama went to great lengths to negotiate this early underlying and foundational site of anger during his first presidential campaign and the first few years of his presidency.

The first of these moments happened during Obama's 2008 presidential campaign after news outlets discovered controversial statements by the president's spiritual leader, Reverend Jeremiah Wright of Trinity Unity Church of Christ in Chicago, Illinois. Obama's spirituality was up for debate by conservative voters. There were routine attacks on Obama's faith and a desire to represent him as a Muslim. In one of these controversial statements, Reverend Wright suggested that the September 11 terror attacks were retribution for a persistent U.S. foreign policy that relied on violence, intimidation, and death to maintain the country's status as a global power. Wright echoed the words of Malcolm X, stating, "We bombed Hiroshima, we bombed Nagasaki, and we nuked far more than the thousands in New York and the Pentagon, and we never batted an eye ... and now we are indignant, because the stuff we have done overseas is now brought back into our own front yards. America's chickens are coming home to roost." Instead of situating the United States as an innocent global player, Wright insinuated that the anger and violence that was perpetrated against the country was part of a continuum of hate and violence.

For the media, Wright was an easy means of connecting Obama to a Black radical theological and political tradition. As noted above, there were persistent attempts to link Obama to the Islamic faith, which in certain corners of the United States was a thinly veiled attempt to link Obama to terrorism. "A More Perfect Union," the speech that Obama gave on the campaign trail at the Constitution Center in Philadelphia on March 2008, was arguably the most impactful during his path to the presidency for the ways it directly addressed issues of race and racism in relationship to his candidacy.[13] He speaks openly about his campaign and subsequent presidency not being a marker of what we now refer to as postracialism. Obama historicized race relations in an attempt to contextualize Reverend Wright's "anger" while at the same time distancing himself and campaign from the bad publicity:

> But for all those who scratched and clawed their way to get a piece of the American Dream, there were many who didn't make it—those who were ultimately defeated, in one way or another, by discrimination. That legacy of defeat was passed on to future generations—those young men and increasingly young women who we see standing on street corners or languishing in our prisons, without hope or prospects for the future. Even for those blacks who did make it, questions of race, and racism, continue to define their worldview in fundamental ways. For the men and women of Reverend Wright's generation, the memories of humiliation and doubt and fear have not gone away; nor has the anger and the bitterness of those years. That anger may not get expressed in public, in front of White co-workers or White friends. But it does find voice in the barbershop or around the kitchen table. At times, that anger is exploited by politicians, to gin up votes along racial lines, or to make up for a politician's own failings. And occasionally it finds voice in the church on Sunday morning, in the pulpit and in the pews. The fact that so many people are surprised to hear that anger in some of Reverend Wright's sermons simply reminds us of the old truism that the most segregated hour in American life occurs on Sunday morning. That anger is not always productive; indeed, all too often it distracts atten-tion from solving real problems; it keeps us from squarely facing our own complicity in our condition, and prevents the African-American community from forging the alli-ances it needs to bring about real change. But the anger is real; it is powerful; and to simply wish it away, to condemn

it without understanding its roots, only serves to widen the chasm of misunderstanding that exists between the races.[14]

Obama cites anger as the underlying feeling that informs Reverend Wright's words, as he links a broader generational feeling of rage as the inevitable response to more overt forms of systemic racism. Obama skillfully describes Wright as part of an angry generation that he is foreclosed to because of his proximity to Jim Crow and argues that it was Wright's inability to hope that kept him from acknowledging the gains made in racial equality in the late twentieth century and envisioning progress/change. Indeed, Obama's articulation of the emotional reverberations of Jim Crow for Black people succinctly illuminates both the despair and anger at centuries of devaluation and dispossession. Obama creates Ahmed's dialectic between anger and hope as seemingly mutually exclusive ideals while simultaneously situating himself as the candidate of hope, and as such he marks himself and his campaign as not a stagnant "static" form of blackness but one that looks forward in its ability to engender change, one inherently different than the angry, older, Black generation that preceded his.[15]

The second key moment was Obama's response to the racially motivated arrest of Harvard professor Henry Louis Gates. Police sergeant James Crowley arrested Gates on July 16, 2009, for breaking into his own home after he returned to Cambridge from a trip abroad. Many felt the arrest was the product of racial profiling, including Gates. Initially, Obama's response to Gates's arrest was somewhat fiery for an even-keeled president. He stated in a press conference, "I think it's fair to say, number one, any of us would be pretty angry; number two, that the Cambridge police acted stupidly in arresting somebody when there was already proof that they were in their own home, and, number three . . . there's a long history in this country of

African Americans and Latinos being stopped by law enforcement disproportionately."[16] This was before the death of Trayvon Martin in 2012 and the founding of the Black Lives Matter movement by Alicia Garza, Opal Tometi, and Patrisse Cullors in 2013. Obama publicly recognized the long-standing history of police brutality and surveillance in communities of color. Unlike his previous admonishment of Reverend Wright's anger, Obama suggested on this occasion that Gates's anger was warranted, but also stated, "I don't know, not having been there and not seeing all the facts, what role race played in that."[17] Although Obama would apologize for his language a few days later and say that this was all around a "teachable moment," the strength of his statement was enough for the Cambridge Police Department to demand an apology from the president. The president invited the arresting officer and Gates to the White House for what is now known as the "Beer Summit."

Less than a year later, political pundits and public opinion demanded the president leave his calm and measured style for a more forceful and angrier style of communication, specifically toward to the executives at BP in response to the 2010 Deepwater Horizon oil spill in the Gulf of Mexico. The spill began after an explosion on April 20 and was not capped until July 15. The country seemingly wanted Obama to engage in a type of innate Black anger and rage that he would perform in our national best interests. It was as if conservatives, environmentalists, and liberals alike realized that Black anger and rage had the potential to be co-opted by the state and could potentially benefit various special interest groups and political parties. While Black scholars, theologians, leaders, and others demanded that Obama be more incensed by matters directly pertaining to Black life throughout his presidency, for the vast majority of Americans the moments for co-opted anger rarely broached issues of race.

In the second year of Obama's first term, conservatives and liberals alike began to focus on the president's previous job as a law school professor at the University of Chicago and to refer to him as "professorial," oftentimes using the word pejoratively to suggest that he was slow to act, overly analytical, and elitist. The political discourse of "the professorial president" illuminated the ways in which Obama did or did not perform affect for public consumption. Critics of the president focusing on his past as a professor and referring to him as professorial to portray him as elitist and out of touch was not new. Indeed, throughout his 2008 campaign Obama was constantly referred to as elitist for his degrees from Columbia and Harvard Law School. Matt Lauer, in an interview about the BP oil spill, exemplified the president's critics by suggesting that he was spending too much time with specialists, not enough time in the Gulf: "I never thought I would say this to a president, but kick some butt." Obama responded by stating, "I don't sit around talking to experts because this is a college seminar. . . . We talk to these folks because they potentially have the best answers, so I know whose ass to kick."[18] Obama, clearly frustrated by this line of criticism and the media's obsession about his affective and emotional responses, adds that "this is not theater."

Obama's "this is not theater" is a suggestion that his emotionality is not performative or dictated. However, politicians' emotionality is routinely critiqued in the public eye. For instance, when the public read then presidential hopeful Howard Dean's excitement at coming in third in the 2004 Iowa Caucus as "too excited" he no longer was a frontrunner in the race, and ultimately did not make it out of the Democratic primary. However, race mediates all of these performances and for Obama, much of his affective performance was through the lens of Black masculine cool posing. As Richard Majors and Janet Billson assert, "Cool pose is a ritualized form of masculinity that entails behaviors, scripts, physical posturing, impression management and carefully crafted performances that deliver a single, critical message: pride, strength, and control."[19] Whether it was singing Al Green or playing basketball on the White House lawn, Obama maintained delicate performances of blackness, often choosing to personify Black masculine coolness or anguish and grief: performances that were palatable and legible by dominant culture. These performances of coolness often moved into the realm of humor. On the *Late Night with Jimmy Fallon* in 2012, the president slow-jammed the news with the help of Fallon and Black Thought, lead singer/ rapper of the neo-soul group The Roots.[20] However, Obama recognized from the outset of his presidency that it was *not* cool for the first Black president to be angry.

The prevalence of private expressions and suppressions of Black masculine anger emanates from corporate, political, and academic spaces and is well represented in contemporary Black satire. The most prominent of these satirical instantiations is from the recurring *Key and Peele* (2012–2015) sketch "Luther the Anger Translator," wherein Keegan-Michael Key and Jordan Peele create an imaginative space that accentuates the muffled anger and rage behind President Obama's calm and measured affect. In addition, the shared biraciality of Obama and Key and Peele can be seen as a site of authority and authenticity as a tool to elucidate the artifice of dominant culture's assumptions about Black masculine emotionality.

When President Obama invited Luther the Anger Translator onstage at the 2015 WHCA annual dinner he stated, "I often joke about tensions between me and the press, but honestly what they say doesn't bother me. I understand we have an adversarial system. I'm a mellow sort of guy" (Figure 4.1). The arrival of Luther (Key) on stage signals to the audience that race is going to be foregrounded in an exaggerated performance of Black masculine anger, something the president has refused to engage in with the press.[21] The recurring *Key and Peele* sketch features President Obama (Peele) giving various primetime presidential addresses to the American people or having interactions with other political figures, with Luther translating his

4.1. Barack Obama bringing Keegan-Michael Key's character Luther the Anger Translator to the 2015 White House Correspondents' Association dinner stage.

veiled political jargon and measured demeanor with slang, expletives, and an over-the-top anger that is completely uncharacteristic of the president. The sketches, which the president admitted he was a fan of, are a mainstay on the show, which bookended Obama's second term. Obama's introduction of Luther at the 2015 WHCA dinner underscores his own political proximity and performance of anger and the ways that he has routinely distanced himself from what could be considered as Black rage.

The WHCA dinner is an annual event dating back to 1914, when reporters had to make appointments to speak with the president or his cabinet members from outside the gates of the White House. The dinner symbolizes the importance of rigorous political journalism in the democratic process and uses levity to assuage the often tense relationship between White House correspondents and the sitting president.[22] The WHCA is responsible for vetting the White House press corps and raising funds for annual scholarships for rising journalists. The event is an amalgamation of politics, Hollywood celebrity, and humor wherein the president delivers a humorous speech that playfully insults political rivals and the media, and usually includes a mid-level comedian who roasts the president and critiques the media.[23]

The annual WHCA dinner signifies one of many ways the state makes space to indulge critique through a type of comedic performance of self-reflexivity. Stated differently, the WHCA dinner organizes a state logic in the form of a national sense of humor that trivializes and polarizes critique. By "performance of self-reflexivity" I mean the way the event allows sitting presidents to attempt to justify policy or decision making through irony, play, and exaggeration. It is often the president's ability to laugh at himself that serves as the barometer of success. Embedded in the president's use of play is a broader performative act of acknowledging critiques that the people in the room have leveled or reported and his synthesizing of those critiques.

The late twentieth-century turn toward humor as an apparatus to level these sociopolitical critiques highlighted the transgressive power of laughter and ridicule, and Obama's raced body and use of humor functions inside of and simultaneously outside of the state apparatus. During Obama's presidency the WHCA dinners centered performances of Black masculinity in the use of humor and the critiques of the state that often relied on the president's deadpan humor, especially around issues of race. While Black performers like Nat King Cole, Duke Ellington, and Aretha Franklin had entertained guests at earlier dinners, the only other Black comedians to work the event before Obama's presidency were Sinbad and Cedric the Entertainer, two comedians known for their universal appeal who, like Bill Cosby, created routines "rooted in constructing commonalities of experience rather than exploring difference."[24] The WHCA dinners during Obama's presidency were bookended by a pair of Black comedians that centered Black progressivism for the event. In 2009, Wanda Sykes became the first Black queer comedienne to headline the annual event, calling immediate attention to Obama's blackness by stating, "The first black president . . . I know you're biracial, but the first black president. It's proud, you know, you're proud to be able to say that, 'the first black president', well that's unless you screw up—then it's going to be what's up with the half-white guy, huh? Who voted for the mulatto?"[25] And in 2016 Larry Wilmore notoriously ended his routine by stating, "So, Mr. President, if I'm going to keep it one hundred: Yo, Barry, you did it, my nigga."[26]

Sykes's and Wilmore's remarks demonstrate the candid ways that Black comedians and humorists made intimate the subject of race and racism at the WHCA dinner for a president who routinely distanced himself from the public discourse on race. and precisely why this dinner took on new meaning during Obama's presidency. Obama often eschewed his close proximity to race throughout his presidency. The WHCA dinner functions at the intersection of history, culture, politics, and news media and any close reading has to incorporate the nuanced and multifaceted ways these various sites converge on the dinner stage. Sykes used the derogatory term "mulatto," which has its origins in a sixteenth-century Spanish word for "mule."[27] It was used as a way to talk about biraciality or mixed-race people that reinforces difference and racial hierarchy, with whiteness being in the position of the horse and blackness being the donkey producing unnatural or illegitimate offspring. In the early twentieth century, the trope of the tragic mulatto featured in African American literature and cinema, with novels like Nella Larsen's *Quicksand* (1928) and *Passing* (1929), and John M. Stahl's film *Imitation of Life* (1934) representing the anxieties of mixed-race people.[28] If we extrapolate from this logic of the mule in mulatto, Sykes's use of the term after her "unless you screw up" implies that Obama could also be the last Black president if his presidency is not a success. Sykes's playful use of Black authenticity demonstrates the ways the media perceived Obama's body and who would lay claim to his presidency.

Similar to the racial familiarity that Sykes demonstrates in her opening lines, seven years later Larry Wilmore would demonstrate a similar racial familiarity when he closed his speech by saying to Obama "you did it my nigga." Prior to Wilmore's remarks towards Obama, he ends his routine with a heartfelt picture of racial progress and what Obama's presidency has meant to him. Wilmore states, "When I was a kid, I lived in a country where people couldn't accept a black quarterback . . . and now, to live in your time, Mr. President, when a black man can lead the entire free world. Words alone do me no justice."[29] Wilmore's use of "Words alone do me no justice," followed by "my nigga" insists that Black people's colloquial use of the N-word was acceptable to articulate the meaning of Obama's presidency to Black people in a post–civil rights America. Indeed, the exchange between ineffability and Wilmore's use of "nigga" evokes a cultural logic that makes the power of Obama's presidency for Black people as inaccessible to White America as the use of "nigga." Wilmore's "my nigga" is a form of endearment between two Black men also becomes a type of call and response on the WHCA dinner stage, wherein Obama had to respond positively either verbally or corporeally to Wilmore to suggest that he was not wrong for using the word. As Wilmore says, "Yo, Berry, you did it my nigga," he does so by bumping his fist against his chest over his heart—an act that signifies Black solidarity in hip-hop culture. The fist bump on the chest dates back to early hip-hop as it takes both the blackness associated with the closed fist popularized during the Black Panther Party and adds bumping it against the chest to suggest a blackness within. Wilmore uses the bump in conjunction with "nigga" to assert authenticity and authority over the word "nigga" and his usage of it. Wilmore's language also embodies this interplay between authenticity and authority when he uses the Black colloquialism "keep it 100" for being honest. Obama reciprocates this Black masculine performative gesture by fist bumping his own chest twice as a positive response to Wilmore. Then the two enter into a handshake-hug that reaffirmed both Wilmore's affirmation and their collective Black masculine performances.

Key and Peele illuminates the racial performance behind Obama's cultural clasp with Wilmore—reserving his handshake-hugs for Black people—in a 2014 sketch titled "Obama Meet & Greet."[30] In the sketch, President Obama (Peele) has just finished a speech and is exiting a room. He has to interact with a procession of people on his way out, wherein the racial identity of the person he meets prompts different affective performances between him and the person. The comedy of the sketch pivots on Obama meeting an unnamed character (Key) who is racially ambiguous, which prompts Obama to be awkward in performing his racial proximity to Key's character. The sketch demonstrates that while Obama is known for his poise and political acumen, there are slippages that happen ostensibly on the subconscious level of his Black masculine performance. It is in these interpersonal corporeal moments that Obama maintains his Black performance. Wilmore and Obama's fist bumps on the chest are within the same axiological performative space as his fist bump with Michele Obama during his 2008 presidential campaign and suggest a Black hipness and downness that only he can inhabit.

Obama speaks for and through his raced body by using deadpan humor as a politically subversive performance, allowing him to undermine the racist cultural and political regimes that attempted to foreclose the first Black president's ability to speak candidly about American racial politics. The WHCA dinner, with its investment in politically charged humor, gave Obama a platform to use his deadpan humor and its subtle satirical implications to play with politics and race in a public forum without backlash. In his 2011 dinner speech, Obama released a "video" of his live birth that used the opening scene from Disney's *Lion King* (1994) where Rafiki presents Simba to the animal kingdom on pride rock.[31] Obama's video clip followed a week after Hawaii released his long-formed birth certificate, a move that effectively ended the birther movement, and Donald Trump's first presidential bid. In 2013, after the success of Steven Spielberg's *Lincoln* (2012),

Obama did a short sketch about Spielberg making a film about Obama where Daniel Day-Lewis, the actor who played Abraham Lincoln in the film, also plays Obama.[32] The sketch pivoted around blackface minstrelsy as Obama playing Day-Lewis playing Obama.

The character Luther the Anger Translator first appeared on the pilot episode of *Key and Peele*, on the eve of Obama's second term in 2012.[33] Throughout his second term Key and Peele would return to the sketch as a way to ventriloquize and excavate the assumed underlying meaning and emotions the president had about various sociopolitical and cultural subjects. Some of the sketches featured multiple "translators"—for Michelle Obama, Malia Obama, or Hilary Clinton. The prominence of the sketches transcended their Comedy Central roots when Obama invited Luther onto the WHCA dinner stage to help translate his remarks at the 2015 dinner.

Returning to the first sketch of the series in early 2012, we see President Obama (Peele) attending to foreign policy, as well as his opposition at home. The sketches are filmed in what is supposed to resemble the oval office. Obama begins the sketch with, "Good evening my fellow Americans. Now, before I begin, I just want to say that I know a lot of people out there seem to think that I don't get angry. That's just not true. I get angry a lot. It's just the way I express passion is different from most. So, just so there's no more confusion we've hired Luther here to be my anger translator."[34] When Luther says "Hi" in a rough, raspy tone, barely opening his mouth, his affect is one of brimming with anger. The ensuing dialogue highlights the difficulties Obama has at the beginning of his second term, with the Republican Party having the majority in both the House and Senate. Peele states, "On the domestic front I just want to say to my critics I hear your voices and I'm aware of your concerns," which Luther translates as, "So maybe if you could chill the hell out for like a second then maybe I could focus on some shit—you know!"[35]

4.2. President Barack Obama (Jordan Peele) and Luther the Anger Translator (Keegan-Michael Key) make their first appearance during the pilot episode of *Key and Peele* (2012).

Luther's translations are always expletive-laden, angry, and performed with big gestures. He wears large ornate rings on each of his fingers, evoking an image of Mr. T (Laurence Ture-aud), the actor best known for his role B.A. Baracus on the 1980s television series *The A-Team* (1983–1987), and Luther keeps his fingers interlocked across his chest when Obama speaks, almost as if he is a gangster standing next to the president. Furthermore, because these are presidential addresses from the Oval Office that are supposed to be the most direct way that a U.S. president can talk to the American people, both Obama and Luther always look directly at the camera. The sketches attack political parties and opposition and foreign leaders but never indict the audience (Figure 4.2).

In relationship to Comedy Central's archetype *Chappelle's Show* and Dave Chappelle's brand of humor, *Key and Peele* did not couch its humor in a similar aesthetic or cultural logic. Whereas Chappelle utilized neo-soul and hip-hop aesthetics to help ground its racial politics as authentically Black, Key and Peele did not attach the show's blackness to other social, cultural, or political spaces that would function as sites of authenticity or authority.

As I wrote in chapter 2, Chappelle used neo-soul as a way to support the brand of blackness he wanted to portray on the sketch comedy show, and in so doing he gave it a political agenda and moral compass that was invested in critiquing the current state of race and racism in order to ultimately improve the lives of Black people. Unlike Chappelle, Key and Peele did not use another site of Black cultural production to lend authenticity and authority to their understanding and use of blackness. This was in part due to the evolution of the internet and the different ways people were consuming media—specifically the rise of YouTube as a platform that Comedy Central would embrace as a way to decentralize the distribution of its sketch comedy shows. Unlike the lesser-known attempts by Comedy Central to recapture the success and edge of *Chappelle's Show*—*Chocolate News* (2008) and *Mind of Mencia* (2008)—*Key and Peele* was able to capitalize on the new racial realities of having Obama in the White House and won two Emmys and a Peabody Award in the process.

Key and Peele's approach to the show's blackness is steeped in their biraciality. Early in the pilot episode, they introduce themselves to the audience and share that they are both biracial. Then they explain that they are both adept at lying because of the varying ways they feel like they have to "dial up" or perform their blackness in predominantly Black spaces. This introduction follows a sketch with Key on the phone with his wife in the street wanting to buy tickets for the theater for her birthday when Peele's character, who is also on the phone, walks up beside him to wait to cross the street. Both men then increasingly add bass and gruff to their voice in order to sound like stereotypical hypermasculine Black men. Key's character starts to pronounce words wrong and use expletives with his wife, a clear departure from the sweet and endearing tone he had before. The sketch ends when Peele's character is able to cross the street. As he walks away, Peele's character says into the phone, "Oh my god, Christian, I almost totally just got mugged right now."[36] Peele's character uses a distinctly higher pitch than he did when he was at the street corner, a pitch that is meant to represent him as an effeminate, Black gay man.

I include this early sketch to demonstrate the ways that *Key and Peele*'s performances of Black masculinity rely on stereotypes. As I demonstrated in chapter 2, *Chappelle's Show* frequently used stereotypes and caricatures to make commentary on contemporary assumptions about blackness. What sets these two shows apart is that *Key and Peele* offered up this representation of blackness without steeping the show's politics in a space of Black nationalist discourse. This is in part the product of the show's connectedness to Obama's second term—Black political structures did not feel the need to announce themselves in the same way because of the broader representation of blackness emanating from the White House.

One of *Key and Peele*'s most popular sketches is "Substitute Teacher," where Mr. Garvey (Key), a teacher in the "inner-city schools" for over twenty years, enters a predominantly White affluent suburban school as a substitute teacher. Mr. Garvey aggressively starts to take attendance and has unique pronunciations of White students' names. Instead of reading popular White names "traditionally," he instead defers to more ethnic pronunciations that shows his close proximity to Black students. The satire of the sketch lies in its ability to decenter whiteness as the default in a scene that many students of color know well while at the same time complicating the way Black men are forced to be discipliners in school environments. The sketch suggests that the harsh discipline that educators at schools that serve low-income students of color feel is the arbiter of good teaching—exemplified in films like *Coach Carter* (2005) and *Lean on Me* (1989)—is ridiculous.[37] Nevertheless, the sketch leaves space for misunderstanding as the viewer never knows if Mr. Garvey is having a problem reading the names. There are certain signposts that he has a robust vocabulary and therefore is very literate. However, the sketch ends with

Mr. Garvey asking if Timothy (Peele) is in the classroom. Timothy, unlike all of the White students, immediately recognizes his name and mispronounces "present." Mr. Garvey conspicuously shares the surname of Marcus Garvey, the founder of the Universal Negro Improvement Association and African Communities League and leader of the Back-to-Africa Movement, and *Key and Peele*'s Mr. Garvey evokes Marcus Garvey's militancy and Black nationalist fervor. The sketch leaves viewers questioning both Mr. Garvey's and Timothy's literacy and intellect in this predominantly White classroom. This diminishes the possibility of decentering whiteness and calling into question the rigid discipline of predominantly Black schools in favor of an easy laugh that subconsciously endorses historical caricatures of the Zip Coon, a dandy figure on the minstrel stage that was meant to show how free Black men with the veneer of education and sophistication spoke in malapropisms and were comically illogical.

Chappelle's Show routinely relied on stereotypes in order to think about the place where Black expression and American racial ideology converge. Similar to *Key and Peele*'s "Substitute Teacher" sketch, Chappelle routinely left room for the type of open interpretation that I discuss in chapter 2, placing stereotypes about literacy and other racist formations just at the edge of his satirical critique. However, Chappelle rooted his show in a neo-soul logic that informed seemingly multivalent sketches that ended with ambiguous laughter. Key and Peele did not commit to this logic and instead allowed for ambivalence and ambiguity to be defining features of the show.

Key and Peele cite their negative reaction to Obama being heckled in Congress and his stoic response as the primary reason they created the sketch series.[38] On September 9, 2009, during a speech about his proposed health care bill, Obama stated that the bill would not cover undocumented immigrants, to which South Carolina republican House member Joe Wilson shouted, "You lie." Key said of the moment, "For him to have that much composure . . . it's like, you don't have to—not after that. It was really a burr in Jordan's saddle," says Key. "He's like, 'C'mon, brother. If there was ever a time to get down to business, do it. How are you going to just put up a finger and keep talking regular?'"[39] Peele goes on to say, "But that's what we love about him, too," says Peele. "He's so even-measured. He's so together. He's almost like Spock." Key and Peele understand the creation of Luther as a necessary intervention on the emotional demands of Obama and his unwavering stoicism. The correlation that Peele draws between Obama and Spock is a chilling one. Within the realm of the *Star Trek*, Spock is half-human and half-Vulcan, and an apt character to once again highlight the role of biraciality for the president. The linking of Spock and Obama demonstrates precisely the terms of Obama's inability to be fully human in the way he presents his emotions—in *Star Trek* Spock is represented as too mechanical in the way he centers logics and lacks emotionality.

Obama and Luther shared the WHCA dinner stage toward the end of the 2015 dinner. Obama begins by acknowledging the ethos for the dinner when he states that "those in the media don't bother him" and that he understands "we have an adversarial system." He then invites Luther on stage to support him against his "adversaries." As in the televised sketch performances before this, Luther comes to the stage with a scowl on his face that marks his performance as aggressive and stereotypically Black before he even says a word. When Luther takes the mic and states, "Hold on to your lily-white butts," he signals to the audience that he is going to talk unapologetically about race in an emotionally unfiltered way. Obama begins his speech by stating, "In our fast-changing world, traditions like the White House Correspondents' dinner are important," which Luther translates as "I mean, really! What is this dinner? And why am I required to come to it? Jeb Bush, do you really want to do this!" Luther immediately cuts through the niceties of the formal dinner to publicly question the usefulness of the occasion. Contrasting Obama's stoic tone and rigid body language, Luther jumps up and down with emotion and points to his chest to make his point. Luther standing side by side with Obama—the two men sharing the same complexion, height, and build—demonstrates in the starkest terms the impossibility of Obama's having the freedom to share his emotional state in this unfiltered way.

As I suggested at the beginning of the chapter, one of the machinations of white supremacy is the co-optation and misreading of Black emotionality—especially Black rage. Integral in this tradition of misreading Black emotionality is the need to render these expressions of rage laughable and comedic whenever possible. It is important to note that Luther's unfiltered emotional response suggests a particular type of emotional autonomy, especially when juxtaposed to Obama's heavily mediated tone and actions. Luther embodies White America's assumptions about Black rage. It is these assumptions in the White imaginary that gives Luther his cultural currency and makes him funny. Luther's scowl evokes Samuel L. Jackson and the intensity that he brings to his roles. Luther's ornate jewelry, masculine bravado, use of expletives and Black dialect borrow from the popular performances of Blaxploitation films. All of Luther's characteristics suggest that he is the culmination of stereotypical sites of Black rage in a post–civil rights White imaginary.

It is these underlying assumptions about Black rage that make Luther and "his antics" funny to the predominantly White WHCA audience. Luther's exaggerated body language and speech are familiar to the White imaginary, but it is the absurdity of attributing those qualities of Black masculine rage to the president of the United States of America that renders the performance hilarious. As the two men stand next to each other, what gets lost in Luther's translation is the centrality of whiteness and how it both creates the need for Obama's stoicism and informs the stereotypical response of Luther's translation. While there is space for the subversive and Black epistemologies in

Luther's translation, it is important to highlight the reason why the translation is needed and what informs his performance.

Although whiteness creates the logic for Key and Peele's popular sketch series, Obama's stoicism and Luther's translations are steeped in Black ways of knowing. Black people who navigate predominantly White spaces recognize that along with code switching and forms of respectability politics, they are also made to feel that they have to police emotions in public spaces. As Brittney Cooper asserts, "Respectability politics are at their core a rage-management project. Learning to manage one's rage by daily tamping down that rage is a response to routine assaults on one's dignity in a world where rage might get you killed or cause you to lose your job."[40] Cooper's attention to the mythos of respectability politics is geared toward the rampant policing of Michelle Obama's body and body language. However, her words elucidate the terms for Black people stifling their emotional responses in White spaces. The anger that informs Luther's translations is a Black rage that has its roots in slavery and embodies the rage that Black people feel toward microaggressions, institutional racism, structural inequality, and other forms of discrimination. This rage is a response to stressors that affect the both mental and physical well-being of Black people.[41] Doctors are starting to connect how discrimination and institutional racism connect to the health disparities for Black people, and Luther's rage clearly exacts both a mental and physical toll. In this way, Luther's use of this rage toward what Obama acknowledges as "the adversarial system" of the media links these sites of discrimination and inequality to how the media has covered his presidency.

The WHCA dinner sketch continues in the following way:

OBAMA: Because despite our differences, we count on the press to shed light on the most important issues of the day.
LUTHER: And we can count on Fox News to terrify old white people with some nonsense! That was ridiculous.

OBAMA: We won't always see eye to eye.

LUTHER: And, CNN, thank you so much for the wall-to-wall Ebola coverage. For two whole weeks, we were one step away from "The Walking Dead." Then y'all got up and just moved on to the next day. That was awesome. Oh, and by the way, if you haven't noticed, you don't have Ebola!

Luther's anger on stage is a reminder that American racial politics intersect with sensationalism to inform how the media covered Obama's presidency. Here, the inclusion of both Fox News and CNN as part of Luther's critique demonstrates the pervasiveness of race informing the "adversarial system." Although Luther performs Black rage within a White imaginary, it is a site of Black expression that is often foreclosed to White people. Therefore, part of the novelty of Luther's translation for Black viewers is his ability to tell White people to their face how they have wronged the first Black president and how race and whiteness informs that wrongdoing. Luther's diatribes were common talking points among Black Obama supporters who were able to see how race undergirded the media's treatment of Obama.

Obama ends the sketch by focusing on arguably the most important issue of his presidency: the environment. After criticizing the news media for sensationalizing issues he had to deal with throughout his presidency, he talks about the issues the country needs to continue to pay attention to after his term is over.

OBAMA: I mean, look at what's happening right now. Every serious scientist says we need to act. The Pentagon says it's a national security risk. Miami floods on a sunny day and instead of doing anything about it, we've got elected officials throwing snowballs in the Senate.

LUTHER: Okay, I think they got it, bro.

OBAMA: It is crazy! What about our kids? What kind of stupid, short-sided irresponsible bull—

LUTHER: Whoa, whoa, whoa, whoa!

Obama is getting visibly angry by this stage, and it is notable that his anger is geared toward environmental issues. It is the same performative anger that the president used in 2010 when responding to the BP oil crisis. Although Luther's translation usually typifies rage toward the underlying racial politics of Obama's presidency—specifically the way that race informs conservative ideology, Obama's desire to get angry about environmental issues serves as a neutral landing site for his rage. Obama's focus on the environment allows him to not implicate whiteness or enact tropes of Black rage in this forced performance of anger. Obama's performance of rage runs Luther off the stage, stating, "And I'm out of here, man. I ain't trying to get into all this." Obama's ability to out-anger Luther is more of a commentary on the desires of the White imaginary and the pressures and impossibilities of the twenty-first-century race man to live up to White America's assumptions about Black emotionality.

Obama recognizes the way that Luther intervenes in these narratives of Black emotionality and White co-optation, so when he brings Luther to the WHCA dinner he looks to subvert this dynamic of American racial politics via an over-the-top performance of Black masculine rage. In this way Obama uses and subverts Black stereotypes as a way to hold a mirror up to America's assumptions about his body and his emotions. Although my focus here is largely on the contrast between Obama's words and Luther's translations, their playful relationship between both signals the broader ways that Black people have to negotiate a sociopolitical and cultural landscape that often tries to deny Black emotionality. Obama's relationship to public performances of anger and rage reiterates what Cooper and others have said about Black women's mischaracterization of being angry and aggressive. Obama's decision to not incorporate the full range of his emotionality shows in an important way that the race man in this twenty-first century moment is not a viable figure to promote to the intricacies of equity and equality. Obama's decision to air on the side of stoicism shows that the race man in this twenty-first century moment does not have equal access to his emotional life in the public sphere while retaining his ability to lead. Obama recognized that American racial politics stifle Black people's feelings—yet simultaneously requires emotions as a litmus test of an affective patriotism.

Conclusion

Beyond the Funny Race Man

THROUGHOUT THIS BOOK, I have shown how Black men use satire to critique the current state of race and gender formations. The Black male characters they create demonstrate the pitfalls of the race man logic in social, cultural, and political spaces. They render racial uplift narratives and the singular leadership of Black men as both unsustainable and undesirable while at the same time acknowledging the internal and external pressure to conform to the figure of the race man. I began this project by meditating on Sherley Anne Williams's words: "Confront Black male writers—with what they have said about themselves."[1] LaMonda Horton-Stallings talks about Paul Beatty's protagonist in *The White Boy Shuffle* as the anti-race man.[2] It is precisely this language of the anti-race man or the antihero that seems to do the work of moving away from what Williams asserted in her essay are the perennial ways that Black men situated themselves as the hero in their own narratives.[3] This project, in short, is a thinking through of what a glacial fall from grace looks like; thinking about the power of wit and humor to begin the work of decentering Black men from the bedlam of racial uplift narratives and respectability politics.

As I have tried to demonstrate throughout this book, this move to oust the race man through satire comes with its own set of problems for satirists and their characters alike. Patriarchy is a resilient force that reimagines itself across multiple terrains and areas. For Black men who are attendant to one aspect of their domination, patriarchy and misogyny will often emerge in other areas. The novels and sketch comedies discussed in the preceding pages, while broaching the subject of vulnerability and interiority, are not without problems. They do not create narrative worlds and visual spaces that are devoid of misogynoir or classism. The shifts that I examine in this text are a small step in transitioning Black masculinity from the fiction of the race man. These texts offer up the power of satire while demonstrating the pitfalls of hypervisibility.

As I stated in the introduction, these hypervisible satirists have largely eschewed imagining Black women's interiority or broadening the scope of their critique by including queer characters and subject matter. John Oliver Killens's 1971 novel *The Cotillion, or, One Good Bull Is Half the Herd* is a rare exception to this paradigm of male-dominated critiques of the social, cultural, and political landscape of Black life in America.[4] The texts discussed here do not offer up the failings of Black men's leadership and the fictions of the race man in order to highlight the ways that the labor and service of Black women has been erased from the archives. If we return to Williams's call to examine what Black men have said about themselves, I have tried to demonstrate here that Black men have said a lot about themselves and the changing landscape of Black masculinity at the beginning of the twenty-first century—by usurping hero narratives with satirical antihero narratives—but those stories and images have avoided or erased certain experiences that would add to the discourse of Black masculinity. Stories about Black men that think through the implications of Black masculinity and sexuality are desperately needed. Unfortunately, Black cis-gendered, heterosexual men rarely enter into introspective and vulnerable spaces with Black gay men.

Furthermore, it is the unflinching individualism of these narratives that is the most troubling aspect of Black men's satirical production. Throughout recent satirical work, Black men continue to rely on the picaresque tradition to go on introspective quests by themselves. The singularity of Black men's experiences in these narrative worlds continues to detach Black men from necessary sites of community and collaboration. It is in the communal where intentional and unintentional forms of patriarchy and misogyny will be upended for Black men. Indeed, the introspection in Black men's satirical writing and cultural production creates the landscape to explore productive modes of vulnerability that can undermine heteropatriarchy. However, a sustained investment in individualism does nothing more than change the terms of the hypervisibility of Black masculinity. For Black masculine satirical expression, this recent move toward individualism and introspection replaces the rugged, hypermasculine performances of Black masculinity with quiet, quirky loners that feel like they are misunderstood by Black communities and a broader American culture. While the quirkiness of Black masculinity offers up new terrains of Black masculine expression that undermine historical articulations of Black men as the personification of cool, this opening up and visibility of varying forms of expression and identity do not, in and of themselves, confront domination and misogynoir.

That said, there are spaces where Black men continue to mine vulnerability and humor to address Black men and masculinity in ways that attend to the erasure of Black women and in service toward more inclusive sites of community. These men continue to eschew configurations of the race man and use their platform or narrative landscape as a way to make space for others.

A key exponent of this approach is Hannibal Buress, who used his stand-up comedy to bring attention to Bill Cosby's rape allegations. On October 16, 2014, Buress told a Philadelphia comedy club, "[Cosby] gets on TV, 'Pull your pants up, black people . . . I can talk down to you because I had a successful sitcom.' Yeah, but you raped women, Bill Cosby, so turn the crazy down a couple notches." As the number of Cosby's accusers grew, many forgot that it was Buress's quip that brought Cosby's alleged rapes back into the public eye. Nevertheless, Buress's joke was profoundly important for the cultural impact that Black comedians have on the stand-up stage and beyond. It relies on a post–civil rights sensibility—one that avoids deference and patri-archal articulations of solidarity (both within his profession as well as within "the race") in order to create a site of Black masculinity that is critical of the past in order to better understand the present moment. While Buress would later go on to say, "This was unex-pected. I didn't want to do that [make headlines]. . . . It wasn't my intention to make this part of a big discussion. It was just some-thing I was doing at that venue right then." Buress's irreverent critique of Cosby simultaneously demonstrates the hypocritical nature of respectability politics and the prevalence of American rape culture while critiquing notions of Black authenticity and authority. Buress's derisive humor toward Cosby reimagines a Black masculine comedic subjectivity in the twenty-first century. Buress is still critiquing the race man figure in highlighting the irony of Cosby telling Black people to be respectable while being a serial rapist, but his approach is one that at least presents itself as steeped in a broader love and commitment for Black people and women and not the product of self-aggrandizement.

In this short bit, Buress is responding to National Associa-tion for the Advancement of Colored People (NAACP) com-memorative event held on May 17, 2004, the fiftieth anniversary of *Brown v. Board of Education*, where Cosby made what is now known as his "Pound Cake Speech."

> I am talking about these people who cry when their son is standing there in an orange suit. Where were you when he was 2? Where were you when he was 12? Where were you when he was 18 and how come you didn't know that he had a pistol? And where is the father? Or who is his father. . . . What part of Africa did this come from? We are not Africans. Those people are not Africans; they don't know a thing about Africa. With names like Shaniqua, Taliqua, and Mohammed and all of that crap, and all of them are in jail.[5]

In the speech Cosby presents himself as a civil rights stalwart, but he castigates poor Black people for nontraditional family structures, mass incarceration, and lack of parenting. He bemoans the absence of self-determination and respectability politics as the cornerstone of Black life, culture, and political ethos. Cosby's diatribe, primarily against poor Black people, fails to recognize the way that institutional racism in the form of unfair policing practices, sentencing mandates, and a continued Black unemployment rate that is usually double that of Whites informs Black life.[6] Instead, his reliance on respectability politics demonstrates the underbelly of Black racial progress narratives.

Respectability politics at its core is a codified form of victim blaming. For Cosby, Black people are primarily incarcerated because of their inclination toward crime and lack of parenting, two problematic stereotypes of blackness that are routed in racist discourse. It is telling that Cosby felt emboldened to give this address at a NAACP event commemorating the fiftieth anniversary of *Brown v. Board of Education*, the Supreme Court ruling that effectively ended segregation and Jim Crow laws across the U.S. South. Moreover, Cosby felt he was taking up the role of the race man in his fiery speech. He felt that he had to galvanize low-income Black people in order for them to live up to the promise of equality, and that in their current state they did not deserve the fruits of equality that his generation and generations before him had worked toward.

Similar to Sidney Poitier's, Cosby's career was built on a sort of integrationist iconography that downplayed race-based humor in favor of a broader, universalism that depicted blackness as commonplace. However, in this early twenty-first-century moment, Cosby, and more importantly his legacy, gets marked as authentically Black, thereby making Buress's assault on his character an assault on Black respectability politics. Buress's dismissal of Cosby as having "the smuggest old black male public persona" and a "Teflon image" speaks directly to how the American imaginary has immortalized

Cosby as "America's Dad." Buress's critique of Cosby is a critique of American rape culture and respectability politics and is one that is deeply committed to poor Black folxs and women. Although Buress uses Cosby's rape allegations as a punchline during a stand-up routine about the permanency and hypocrisy of respectability politics, he is serious about the rape allegations and implores the audience to do their research. He frequently asks the audience to google the allegations and how those allegations are more prominent, even in their obscurity, than his career.

Jerrod Carmichael's *Home Videos* (2019) and *Sermon on the Mount* (2019) also illuminate the possibility of Black men being vulnerable and introspective to embrace more communal and Black feminist spaces.[7] Carmichael is best known for *The Carmichael Show* (2015–2017) and his two HBO comedy specials *Love at the Store* (2014) and *8* (2017).[8] *Home Videos* and *Sermon on the Mount* are compendiums on the comedian's family life as he thinks through his father's infidelity and his mother's decision to stay with him. However, the series of casual conversations with family members also lets the audience know how this southern Black family thinks through gender, race, love, religion, and sexuality. The personal is political for Carmichael. *Home Videos* premiered on Mother's Day, May 12, 2019, on HBO. The twenty-seven-minute video focuses on conversations with the Black women in Carmichael's family about the role of race, gender, and beauty standards. While not satirical, Carmichael incorporates a kind of humor and vulnerability that lets the viewer into intimate and personal spaces. He is a comedian, so the dialogue and his contribution are often comedic in nature, allowing for these conversations to be serious but also light. *Home Videos* unapologetically opens up space for Black women to tell their stories while simultaneously opening up new terrain to think through sexuality. Carmichael shares that he has "hooked up with guys before" as he pushes his mother to connect more with her sexuality in the wake of his father's infidelity. Although Carmichael shares this part of his personal life casually, such an admission at the outset of the project is important for the ways that it disrupts narratives of heterosexuality and the cool posing of Black funny men. Ultimately, *Home Videos* is Carmichael using his hypervisibility to bring awareness about the worldview of Black women and the significance of their experiences.

Carmichael's *Sermon on the Mount* follows up the space and platform he created for the Black women in his life in *Home Videos* with a deep exploration of his father's infidelity and the notions of masculinity held by those around him. *Sermon on the Mount* is twice as long as *Home Videos* and begins with Carmichael spending time with the men in his family. In conversations with his uncle, cousins, and eventually his father, we see a worldview that attempts to make sense of infidelity, love, and fatherhood. The video begins with a reverend who is close friends with Carmichael's father, counseling Carmichael's mother about the role of forgiveness in their marriage. After the admission of infidelity that Carmichael candidly presents in *Home Videos*, the audience recognizes that this early conversation about forgiveness is in response to her husband's infidelity and extramarital children. The video is bookended with a follow-up conversation between Carmichael's adult sister, mother, and the reverend to talk about the father's infidelity. Without naming it, Carmichael's videos are about gender identity and formation for this Black family in Winston Salem, North Carolina. Within literary circles, writers like Kiese Laymon and others have unapologetically centered vulnerability in their satirical and nonsatirical work in ways that embrace Black women and communities even as they work on Black men's inner mental and emotional lives. Black women are starting to gain more visibility in comedic and satirical spaces. The meteoric rise of Issa Rae is a testament that Black women are making inroads in Black comedic storytelling. Rae's HBO show *Insecure* (2016–) has created a comedic landscape that is deeply committed to showing the fullness of young Black life, with particular attention to gender formations for both Black women and men.[9] The first season of *Insecure*, loosely based on her web series *The Mis-Adventures of Awkward Black Girl* (2011–2013) used humor and directness to articulate the expansiveness of Black gender expression.[10] Specifically, the television show illuminates how the pressures of finding a career, housing, and friendships for young adults manifest themselves in their personal relationships and subsequently how they imagine themselves as Black men and women. By the end of the first season *Insecure* had divided audience members divided on if they should support Issa's character or her boyfriend on the television show. Black women cultural producers offer salient satirical critiques of Black masculinity. With *Insecure*, Rae adds the discourse of "fuckboy," someone who gets away with harmful or negligent behavior because people think he is a good guy, as a necessary critique of Black masculinity. Radha Blank's viral music video "Hotep Hoteppin" similarly critiques Black men's use of Black nationalism as a site of misogynoir.[11]

Beyond these Black women's treatment of more hegemonic forms of Black masculinity, there is an emergence of Black women's comedic and satirical voices. Jessica Williams and Phoebe Robinson's podcast-turned-HBO special *2 Dope Queens* (2016–2018) and Robin Thede's *The Black Lady Sketch Show* (2019–) are disrupting the permanency of Black men telling stories about race and racism for a national stage.[12] The role of HBO and Netflix in democratizing satiric representation cannot be understated. These networks provide a number of opportunities to Black women storytellers, and they reshape a long-standing assumption about Black men's prowess in using humor to make meaning of social difference. In these new television shows, Black women attend to the intersection of race and gender in new and exciting ways that broaden the audience's awareness about the mundane effects of racism and sexism.

Acknowledgments

THIS PROJECT, LIKE all projects, only came to fruition with the unwavering love and support of family, friends, and colleagues. Without the love, laughter, and grace from my wife, Johnnjalyn Manning, this project would not have been possible. She is the first person I go to with an idea and the last person I go to make sure I am making sense. I would also like to thank our children Isaiah, Jaden, and Zuri who have been equally as patient and generous with my writing. A number of scholars that examine Black masculinity oftentimes cite their children as the primary impetus for doing this work. I am no exception. My children have had an immeasurable impact on my thoughts on masculinity and the power of vulnerability and tenderness to replace intergenerational trauma with new modes of love and care.

Played Out is a testament to the fact that I am loved and supported and that I love and support others—I am deeply grateful that these are people I call family. Although he will not read this in his earthly form, the first person I must acknowledge is my grandfather, Edward J. Manning. It was our Sunday conversations talking expansively about Black folks and Black things that ignited a love for Black cultural production and expression. I am also indebted to the grandmother I affectionately call Mama Georgia because she was the most avid reader I saw growing up. Unknowingly, she showed me the pleasure of reading and this project would not have happened if she hadn't passed this along to me. I have to also thank my father because I first watched Chris Rock's *Bigger and Blacker* with him and it clearly left an indelible mark on me and my understanding of Black men, performance, and comedic spaces. Most importantly, my mother had me question from a very early age masculinity and manhood and what kind of man I was going to be. As a single mother, often embracing an inbetweenness of gender roles to raise my brothers and me, she showed me the contours of Black gender performance.

My time at Jackson State University afforded me a glimpse of the Black professoriate and academic life that has sustained me throughout my years in the Academy. Specifically, I would like to thank Loria Brown, Wanda Macon, Jean Chamberlain, and Preselfannie McDaniels and the English Department at Jackson State University for showing me the importance of teaching and mentorship at the undergraduate level. Dr. Macon's courses and her guidance during my extended research project enabled me think of myself as a researcher for the first time—and I deeply appreciate her patience and care throughout that process.

At Ohio State University, I had the pleasure of working with wonderful graduate students and faculty members who deeply informed my thinking around race, gender, and performance. I was fortunate when I first got to Ohio State to have a wonderful cohort of African Americanists in Tayo Clyburn, Candice Pipes, and Tiffany Anderson who were wonderful peer mentors and friends. If I ever had a question, they made themselves available and it was our early conversation about African American literature that helped to shape my move toward satire and my focus on masculinity. Peers such as J. Brendan Shaw, Leila Ben-Nasir, Tiffany Salter, Kate Parker Horigan, Bradley Freeman, Christopher Lewis, Anne Langendorfer, Corinne Martin, Julia Istomina, Toni Calbert, James Harris, and Amber Camus have served as the best academic community a person could ask for. My advisor, Adélékè Adéẹ̀kọ́ is a life force for this project and has been the perfect mentor throughout this journey. Similarly, I deeply appreciate the early guidance and mentorship of Andrea Williams during this project. She has shown me the rigor, professionalism, and kindness that are possible as a mentor in the Academy. I would also like to thank Ryan Freedman, Valerie Lee, Koritha Mitchell, and Simone Drake as early interlocutors and mentors for this project. I am grateful too to LaMonda Horton-Stallings, who has always supported this work and lent her expertise to push it to new heights. Her work and feedback have been deeply informative throughout this process.

The community of scholars at my first job, the University of Nevada, Las Vegas, thoroughly helped advance my thinking on this project. Colleagues like Sheila Bock, A. B. Wilkinson, Ranita Ray, Georgiann Davis, Addie Rolnick, Javon Johnson, Gloria Wong, Suzy Newbury, Rachel J. Anderson, John Hay and Jessica Teague helped to cultivate academic spaces on and off campus where I could ruminate about the exchange between race, gender, and humor. Of all of these colleagues, Mark Padoongpatt and Anita Revilla were the most gracious with their time and helped me form the most salient models of scholarship, pedagogy, and service. Specifically, Mark's unwavering friendship and investment in me and this project has been invaluable. From our late-night writing sessions at Starbucks to bouncing ideas at conferences, our conversations transformed this project from early ideas into what it is today.

This book is also the product of the Woodrow Wilson Career Enhancement Fellowship. It is also important that in graduate school I attended a National Endowment for the Humanities Summer Institute at Pennsylvania State University under the tutelage of the late Lovalerie King. The space she created over a few weeks during my formative graduate years helped set a trajectory for me as a scholar and this text as a manuscript. I'm deeply indebted to her for creating such a generative space for African Americanist. I am thankful for Kerry Haynie and the Summer Institute on Tenure and Professional

Advancement. This early program helped to provide me necessary mentorship and supported this project.

At Texas Christian University, I have had a number of colleagues be supportive of this project. I am thankful for the support and care from Theresa Gaul, Sarah Robbins, Karen Steele, Gabi Kirillof, Alex Lemon, Joddy Murray, Jason Helms, Ariane Balizet, David Colon, Bonnie Blackwell, Charlotte Hogg, Mona Norain, and Joseph Darda. I am especially appreciative of the space that Stacie McCormick, Rima Abunasser, Jeanelle Hope, Jane Mantey, and Carmen Kynard create on campus every day. They have supported me and in turn have supported this project.

Outside of my university affiliations, I am indebted to colleagues Julius Fleming, Jeffrey Coleman, Briana Whiteside, Darryl Dickson-Carr, Lisa Guerrero, Rhaisa Williams, David Green, Regina Bradley, La Marr Bruce, Darius Bost, Ryan Sharp, Jervette Ward, Candice Jenkins, Kameelah Martin. Mentors such as Robert Patterson, Soyica Diggs Colbert, GerShun Avilez, Theri Pickens, Rebecaa Wanzo, Herman Beavers, and Jeffrey McCune. In short, I'm deeply grateful for my family, friends, and community. a Adélékè Adéèkó imparted an important Ghanaian proverb early in my career: "If a needle really could sew, it wouldn't have a hole on its back." This project, like all projects, is a tapestry that is indebted to both the needle and thread and the community they create together. Thank you.

Notes

Introduction

1. Kendrick Lamar, *To Pimp a Butterfly*, Aftermath Entertainment, Interscope Records, and Top Dawg Entertainment, 2015, compact disc.
2. Kendrick Lamar featuring U2, "XXX," track 11 on *Damn*, Aftermath Entertainment, Interscope Records, and Top Dawg Entertainment, 2017, compact disc.
3. The idea that God would only bless those that America is good to is easily understood as a neoliberal articulation of patriotism, faith, and economic success. The lyrics in "XXX" further highlight this paradigm when Lamar raps, "Hail Mary, Jesus and Joseph / The great American flag / Is wrapped and dragged with explosives / Compulsive disorder, sons and daughters / Barricaded blocks and borders / Look what you taught us / It's murder on my street, your street, back streets / Wall street, corporate offices, banks / Employees and bosses with homicidal thoughts."
4. Christina Sharpe, *In the Wake: On Blackness and Being* (Durham: Duke University Press, 2016), 8.
5. A griot is a traveling storyteller in parts of West Africa.
6. Charles A. Knight, *The Literature of Satire* (Cambridge: University of Cambridge Press, 2004), 15.
7. I mention both Bert Williams and Charles Chesnutt here for the ways that they were popular Black humorists at the turn of the century. Williams and Chesnutt's popularity was tied to their use of stereotypical images of blackness. Both Williams as a blackface minstrel performer and Chesnutt as a writer that used southern Black dialect grew their popularity through White America's nostalgia for plantation life in the post-Bellum era. See Charles Chesnutt, *The Conjure Woman and Other Conjure Tales* (Durham, NC: Duke University Press, 1993).
8. Vincent Woodard, *The Delectable Negro: Human Consumption and Homoeroticism with U.S. Slave Culture* (New York: New York University Press, 2014), 18.
9. Michael Billig, *Laughter and Ridicule: Towards a Social Critique of Humour* (London: SAGE, 2005), 9.

10. Jose Munoz, *Disidentifications: Queers of Color and the Performance of Politics* (Minneapolis: University of Minnesota Press, 2013).
11. Fred Moten, *In the Break: The Aesthetics of the Black Radical Tradition* (Minneapolis: University of Minnesota Press, 2003), 1.
12. Northrop Frye, *Anatomy of Criticism: Four Essays* (Princeton, NJ: Princeton University Press, 1957), 224.
13. Darryl Dickson-Carr, *African American Satire: The Sacredly Profane Novel* (Columbia: University of Missouri Press, 2001), 3.
14. Christina Sharpe, *Monstrous Intimacies: Making Post-Slavery Subjects* (Durham, NC: Duke University Press, 2010), 4.
15. Paul Beatty, "Introduction," in *Hokum: An Anthology of African-American Humor*, ed. Paul Beatty (New York: Bloomsbury, 2006), 2.
16. Chris Jackson, "Our Thing: An Interview with Paul Beatty," *Paris Review*, May 7, 2015.
17. Viveca S. Green, "'Deplorable' Satire: Alt-Right Memes, White Genocide Tweets, and Redpilling Normies," *Studies in American Humor* 5, no. 1: 31–69.
18. I use "Black satire" instead of "African American satire" as both a way to be more inclusive of the diaspora in my language as well as in an attempt to resist the class and respectable implications of the descriptor African American.
19. Dustin Griffin, *Satire: A Critical Reintroduction* (Lexington: University Press of Kentucky, 1994), 133.
20. Alain Locke, *The New Negro* (Salem, NH: Ayer Company, 1986), 7.
21. George S. Schuyler, "The Negro-Art Hokum," *Nation* 122 (June 16, 1926): 662–663.
22. George Schuyler, *Black No More* (New York: Macaulay Co., 1931).
23. Wallace Thurman, *Infants of the Spring* (New York: Macaulay Co., 1932).
24. Darryl Dickson-Carr, *Spoofing the Modern: Satire in the Harlem Renaissance* (Columbia: University of South Carolina Press, 2015), 116.
25. Ralph Ellison, *Invisible Man* (New York: Random House, 1952).
26. This is a phenomenon that Michele Wallace argues is the pivot from modernism to postmodernism, from invisibility to hypervisibility around Black culture in African American literature in *Dark Designs and Visual Cultures* (Durham, NC: Duke University Press, 2004), 370–371.
27. Mat Johnson, *Pym* (New York: Spiegel & Grau, 2011).
28. Edgar Allen Poe, *The Narrative of Arthur Gordon Pym of Nantucket* (New York: Harper & Brothers, 1838).
29. Toni Morrison, *Playing in the Dark: Whiteness and the Literary Imagination* (Cambridge, MA: Harvard University Press, 1992).
30. Mat Johnson, *Pym* (New York: Spiegel and Grau, 2011), 14.
31. Ishmael Reed, *Flight to Canada* (New York: Simon & Schuster, 1976).
32. Harriet Beecher Stowe, *Uncle Tom's Cabin* (Boston: John P. Jewett and Co., 1852).
33. Sam Greenlee, *The Spoke Who Sat by the Door* (London: Allison & Busby, 1969); John Oliver Killens, *The Cotillion, or, One Good Bull*

Is Half the Herd (Trident Press, 1971); Ishmael Reed, *Mumbo Jumbo* (New York: Doubleday, 1972); and Fran Ross, *Oreo* (New York: Greyfalcon House 1974).

34. Richard Pryor, *The Richard Pryor Show* (Burbank, CA: NBC Studios, 1977).
35. Trey Ellis, *Platitudes* (New York: Vintage Books, 1988); Darius James, *Negrophobia: An Urban Parable* (Secaucus, NJ: Carol Publishing Group, 1992); Paul Beatty, *The White Boy Shuffle* (Boston: Houghton Mifflin Harcourt, 1996); Shawn Wayans, Marlon Wayans, and Phil Beauman, *Don't Be a Menace in South Central while Drinking Your Juice in the Hood*, Island Pictures and Ivory Way Productions, film (1996); and Keenen Ivory Wayans, *In Living Color* (Hollywood, CA: 20th Century Fox Television, 1990–1994).
36. Robert Townsend and Keenen Ivory Wayans, *Hollywood Shuffle*, Conquering Unicorn, film (1987); George C. Wolfe, *The Colored Museum* (New York: Grove Press, 1987); Chris Rock, Nelson George, and Robert LoCash, *CB4*, Imagine Entertainment and Universal Studios, film (1993); and Chris Rock, *The Chris Rock Show*, HBO, (1997–2000).
37. Percival Everett, *Erasure* (Minneapolis: Graywolf Press, 2001); Spike Lee, *Bamboozled*, New Line Cinema and 40 Acres & A Mule Filmworks, film (2000).
38. damali ayo, *How to Rent a Negro* (Chicago: Lawrence Hill Books, 2005).
39. Alice Walker, *The Color Purple* (San Diego: Harcourt Press, 1982).
40. Ishmael Reed, *Reckless Eyeballing* (New York: Dalkey Archive Press, 2000).
41. Reed, *Reckless Eyeballing*, 4.
42. Ellis, *Platitudes*.
43. Alice Walker, *The Color Purple* (New York: Harcourt Brace Jovanovich, 1982).
44. Sapphire, *Push* (New York: Vintage Books, 1996).
45. Mark Marvel interview with Sapphire, "Sapphire's Big Push—Sapphire's novel, 'Push,'" June 20, 2021, https://indexarticles.com/arts/interview/sapphires-big-push-sapphires-novel-push/.
46. Wolfe, *The Colored Museum*.
47. Eldridge Cleaver, *Souls On Ice* (New York: Delta Publishing, 1968).
48. Wolfe, *Colored Museum*, 33.
49. At the heart of *Soul on Ice*, Cleaver muses about how Black men have been feminized and how a reclamation of Black masculinity is going to counteract systems of domination that constantly marginalize people of color (155–175).
50. Moya Bailey and Trudy, "On Misogynoir: Citation, Erasure, and Plagiarism," *Feminist Media Studies* 18, no. 4 (2018): 762–768.
51. Bailey and Trudy, "On Misogynoir," 762.
52. Christopher Hitchens, "Why Women Aren't Funny," *Vanity Fair*, January 2007, https://www.vanityfair.com/culture/2007/01/hitchens200701.

53. Ann Oldenburg, "Kenan Thompson: Black Female Comics Not 'Ready' for 'SNL,'" *USA Today*, October 15, 2013, https://www.usatoday.com/story/life/people/2013/10/15/kenan-thompson-black-comediennes-snl-lacking-diversity/2988663/.

54. Linda Mizejewski, *Pretty/Funny: Women Comedians and Body Politics* (Austin: University of Texas Press 2015), 6.

55. Knight, *Literature of Satire*, 7.

56. Dickson-Carr, *African American Satire*.

57. Simone Drake, *When We Imagine Grace: Black Men and Subject Making* (Chicago: University of Chicago Press, 2016), 3.

58. When *Played Out* uses "vulnerability," it is to suggest how Black men should embrace and move toward an emotional and psychological vulnerability—one that undermines patriarchal formations, not supports them.

59. Judith Butler, Zeynep Gambetti, and Leticia Sabsay, *Vulnerability in Resistance* (Durham, NC: Duke University Press, 2016), 7.

60. Hortense Spillers, "Mama's Baby, Papa's Maybe: An American Grammar Book," *Diacritics* 17, no. 2 (Summer 1987): 80.

61. Sherley Ann Williams, "Some Implications of a Womanist Theory," *Callaloo* 9, no. 2 (Spring 1986): 307.

62. Paul Beatty, *The Sellout* (New York: Picador, 2016); Dave Chappelle and Neal Brennan, *Chappelle's Show* (New York, NY: Comedy Central and Pilot Boy Productions, 2003–2006); Percival Everett, *I Am Not Sidney Poitier* (Saint Paul: Graywolf Press, 2009); and Keegan-Michael Key and Jordan Peele, *Key and Peele* (Monkeypaw Productions and Martel & Roberts Productions, 2012–2015).

63. Roderick Ferguson, *The Reorder of Things: The University and Its Pedagogies of Minority Difference* (Minneapolis: University of Minnesota Press, 2012).

64. Jay Z, *Decoded* (New York: Spiegel and Grau, 2010), 18.

65. E. Patrick Johnson, *Appropriating Blackness: Performance and the Politics of Authenticity* (Durham: Duke University Press, 2003).

66. W. E. B. Du Bois, *The Souls of Black Folk: A Norton Critical Edition*, ed. Henry Louis Gates Jr. and Terri Hume Oliver (New York: W. W. Norton, 1999).

CHAPTER I   OF OUR SATIRICAL STRIVINGS

Epigraph: James Baldwin and Audre Lorde, "Revolutionary Hope: A Conversation between James Baldwin and Audre Lorde," *Essence* 15, no. 8 (December 1984): 72.

1. Imani Perry, *Vexy Thing: On Gender and Liberation* (Durham, NC: Duke University Press, 2018).

2. W.E.B. Du Bois, *The Souls of Black Folk: A Norton Critical Edition*, ed. Henry Louis Gates Jr. and Terri Hume Oliver (New York: W. W. Norton, 1999), 39.

3. Du Bois, *Souls of Black Folk*, 16.

4. Rinaldo Walcott, "Reconstructing Manhood; or, the Drag of Black Masculinity," *Small Axe* 13, no. 1 (March 2009): 75–89. As Walcott observes, "The masks black men wear are many and varied and might be understood as congruent with the difficult history of the agency or lack thereof of black masculine self-fashioning that is autonomous and wholly self-interested" (75).

5. Erica Edwards, *Charisma and the Fictions of Black Leadership* (Minneapolis: University of Minnesota Press, 2012), 6.

6. Du Bois, *Souls of Black Folk* (speech for women suffrage).

7. Du Bois, *Souls of Black Folk*, 10–11.

8. Hazel Carby, *Race Men* (Cambridge, MA: Harvard University Press, 1998).

9. Brittney Cooper, *Beyond Respectability: The Intellectual Thought of Race Women* (Urbana: University of Illinois Press, 2017).

10. Erica Edwards, *Charisma*, 21.

11. Du Bois, *Souls of Black Folk*, 16.

12. Du Bois, *Souls of Black Folk*, 11.

13. Du Bois, *Souls of Black Folk*, 11.

14. Paul Gilroy, *The Black Atlantic: Modernity and Double-Consciousness* (Cambridge, MA: Harvard University Press, 1993), 37.

15. Robert Patterson, *Exodus Politics: Civil Rights and Leadership in African American Literature and Culture* (Charlottesville: University of Virginia Press, 2013), 137.

16. Cornel West, *Race Matters* (New York: Vintage, 1994), 19.

17. West, *Race Matters*, 22–23.

18. West, *Race Matters*, 24.

19. Calvin Warren, "Black Nihilism and the Politics of Hope," *New Centennial Review* 15, no. 1 (2015): 221.

20. Friedrich Nietzsche, *The Will to Power* (New York: Vintage, 1968).

21. West, *Race Matters*, 23.

22. Nietzsche, *Will to Power*, 4.

23. Paul Beatty, *The Sellout* (New York: Farrar, Straus and Giroux, 2015).

24. Paul Beatty, "Introduction," in *Hokum: An Anthology of African-American Humor*, ed. Paul Beatty (New York: Bloomsbury, 2006), 2.

25. The "post-soul," as I asserted in the introduction, is the site in which Black subjectivity, is irreverent to a history of racial progress to distance present sensibilities and aestheticisms from a pre–civil rights epoch that represents the continued social, cultural, and political impetus to strive toward emancipation and equality.

26. Paul Beatty, *The White Boy Shuffle* (New York: Houghton Mifflin, 1996).

27. Du Bois, *Souls of Black Folk*, 10.
28. A palimpsest is generally acknowledged with medieval presses when the text is erased and written over, but still leaves traces of the original in the creation of something new. I use palimpsest as a way of articulating the way Beatty evokes civil rights iconography and narratives and then subverts them.
29. Chris Jackson, "Our Thing: An Interview with Paul Beatty," *Paris Review*, May 7, 2015, 6.
30. Nicole Fleetwood, *Troubling Vision: Performance, Visuality, and Blackness* (Chicago: University of Chicago Press, 2011), 33.
31. Alexander Blackburn, *The Myth of the Picaro: Continuity and Transformation of the Picaresque Novel, 1554–1954* (Chapel Hill: University of North Carolina Press, 1979), 19.
32. Darryl Dickson-Carr, *African American Satire: The Sacredly Profane Novel* (Columbia: University of Missouri Press, 2001), 36.
33. Blackburn, *Myth of the Picaro*, 20.
34. Percival Everett, *Erasure* (Hanover: University Press of New England, 2001); Spike Lee, *Bamboozled*, New Line Cinema and 40 Acres & Mule Filmworks, film (2000); Aaron McGruder, *The Boondocks*, https://www.gocomics.com/boondocks, June 2, 2021; and Mat Johnson, *Pym* (New York: Spiegel & Grau, 2011).
35. Judith Butler, *Precarious Life: The Powers of Mourning and Violence* (London: Verso, 2004).
36. Dickson-Carr, *African American Satire*, 36.
37. "Paul Beatty by Rone Shavers," *BOMB*, no. 72 (July 1, 2000), https://bombmagazine.org/articles/paul-beatty/.
38. Richard Pèrez-Pena, "Woman Linked to 1955 Emmett Till Murder Tells Historian Her Claims Were False," *New York Times*, January 27, 2017, https://www.nytimes.com/2017/01/27/us/emmett-till -lynching-carolyn-bryant-donham.html.
39. *Jet Magazine* 8, no. 19 (September 15, 1955): 9.
40. William Cross Jr., "The Negro-to-Black Conversion Experience," *Black World* 20, no. 9 (1971): 13–27.
41. Cross Jr., "Negro-to-Black Conversion Experience," 23.
42. Derrick Bell, "Space Traders" in *Faces in the Bottom of the Well* (New York: Basic Books, 1992), 158–194; Sam Greenlee, *The Spoke Who Sat by the Door* (London: Allison & Busby, 1969); Ishmael Reed, *Flight to Canada* (New York: Random House, 1976); and Spike Lee, *Bamboozled*, New Line Cinema and 40 Acres & Mule Filmworks, film (2000).
43. Lisa Guerrero, *Crazy Funny: Popular Black Satire and the Method of Madness* (New York: Routledge, 2020), 164.

Chapter 2   Neoliberalism and the Funny Race Man

1. Wahneema Lubiano, "Black Nationalism and Black Common Sense: Policing Ourselves and Others," in *The House That Race Built*, ed. Wahneema Lubiano (New York: Vintage, 1997), 232.

2. Marlon Riggs, "Black Macho Revisited: Reflections of a SNAP! Queen," in *Black Men on Race, Gender, and Sexuality: A Critical Reader*, ed. Devon Carbado (New York: New York University Press, 1999); E. Patrick Johnson, *Appropriation Blackness* (Durham, NC: Duke University Press, 1999); Damon Wayans and David Alan Grier, "Men on Film," *In Living Color*; Keenen Ivory Wayans, *In Living Color* (Hollywood, CA: 20th Century Fox Television, 1990–1994).

3. Nick Marx, *Sketch Comedy: Identity, Reflexivity, and American Television* (Bloomington: Indiana University Press, 2019), 2–3.

4. Richard Pryor, *The Richard Pryor Show* (Burbank, CA: Burt Sugarman Productions, 1977); Wayans, *In Living Color* (1990–1994); Chris Rock, *The Chris Rock Show*, HBO, 1997–2000; Dave Chappelle and Neal Brennan, *Chappelle's Show* (New York, NY: Comedy Central and Pilot Boy Productions, 2003–2006); Comedy Central, http://www.cc.com/shows/chappelle-s-show.

5. Dave Chappelle and Neal Brennan, *Half Baked*, Robert Simonds Production and Universal Pictures, film, 1998.

6. Bambi Haggins, "In the Wake of 'The Nigger Pixie,'" in *Satire TV: Politics and Comedy in the Post-Network Era*, ed. Jonathan Gray and Jeffrey Jones (New York: New York University Press, 2009), 207; Haggins convincingly locates Chappelle's "down-ness," or coolness, as the primary factor in his rise to fame. Thus, her articulation deconstructs Comedy Central's continuing claim that *Chappelle's Show* is a "social phenomenon."

7. *Iconoclasts*, series 2, episode 6, "Dave Chappelle and Maya Angelou," dir. Joe Berlinger, aired November 30, 2006, on Sundance Channel.

8. Nelson George, *Hip Hop America* (New York: Penguin, 1998).

9. Mark Anthony Neal, *Post-Soul Babies: Black Popular Culture and the Post-Soul Aesthetic* (New York: Routledge, 2002), 3.

10. In the DVD audio commentary, Chappelle explains that his Black friend is Cey Adams, a hip-hop visual artist who created many of Def Jam's early album covers. During the conversation, Brennan quotes Adams as later saying, "People will laugh at anything." Chappelle also mentions that the idea for the sketch came from his grandfather, a blind man who was either white or light enough to pass but was raised Black in Washington, DC. The anecdote is another example of Chappelle's tendency to make himself vulnerable by sharing personal experiences with his viewers; *Chappelle's Show*, season 1, episode 1, "Clayton Bigsby," dir. Rusty Cundieff, DVD.

11. D. W. Griffith, Thomas Dixon Jr., and Frank E. Woods, *The Birth of a Nation*, David W. Griffith Corp. and Epoch Producing Company, film (1915), Charles J. Correll and Freeman F. Gosden, *Amos 'n' Andy* (Culver City, CA: Hal Roach Studios, 1928–1960).

12. W.E.B. Du Bois, "Criteria of Negro Art," *Crisis* 32 (October 1926): 290–297.

13. Sigmund Freud, *Jokes and Their Relation to the Unconscious* (New York: W. W. Norton, 1960), 107.

14. Michael Billig, *Laughter and Ridicule: Towards a Social Critique of Humour* (London: SAGE, 2005), 211.

15. Rebecca Krefting, *All Joking Aside: American Humor and Its Discontents* (Baltimore: Johns Hopkins University Press, 2014), 180.

16. Ralph Ellison, "Change the Joke and Slip the Yoke," *Partisan Review* 25, no. 2 (1958): 55.

17. *Chappelle's Show*, season 2, episode 2, "The Niggar Family," dir. Rusty Cundieff, aired January 28, 2004, on Comedy Central.

18. Danielle Fuentes Morgan, *Laughing to Keep From Dying: African American Satire in the Twenty-First Century* (Urbana: University of Illinois Press, 2020), 2.

19. *Iconoclasts*, series 2, episode 6.

20. Christopher Farley, "Dave Speaks," *Time*, May 23, 2005, 68.

21. In many ways, the scene echoes the two jive-talking Black men in the 1980 film *Airplane!* When the flight attendant asks what they want for their inflight meal, they respond by speaking jive as if it were a separate language. The move seemingly embraces stereotypical representations of Black men as the epitome of cool.

22. *Chappelle's Show*, season 3, episode 2, "Black Howard Dean & Stereotype Pixies," dir. Rusty Cundieff, aired July 16, 2006, on Comedy Central.

23. Saidiya Hartman, *Scenes of Subjection: Terror, Slavery, and Self-Making in Nineteenth-Century America* (Oxford: Oxford University Press, 1997).

24. *Chappelle's Show*, season 3, episode 2.

25. *MTV Cribs* is a television show about prominent young artists, athletes, other celebrities who give tours of their homes and other assets. The show began airing in 2000.

26. *Chappelle's Show*, season 3, episode 2.

27. Eric Lott, *Love and Theft: Blackface Minstrelsy and the American Working Class* (Oxford: Oxford University Press, 1993), 3–4.

28. Michael Rogin, *Blackface, White Noise: Jewish Immigrants in the Hollywood Melting Pot* (Berkeley: University of California Press), 22.

29. Lott, *Love and Theft*.

30. Daphne Brooks, *Bodies in Dissent: Spectacular Performances of Race and Freedom, 1850–1910* (Durham, NC: Duke University Press, 2006), 63.

31. Devin Gordon, "Dave Chappelle: Fears of a Clown," *Newsweek*, May 16, 2005, 60.

32. Lott, *Love and Theft*, 142.

33. Lott, *Love and Theft*, 20.

34. Maurice Manring, *Slave in a Box: The Strange Career of Aunt Jemima* (Charlottesville: University of Virginia Press, 1998).

35. Robert Nevin, "Stephen C. Foster and Negro Minstrelsy," *Atlantic* 20, no. 121 (November 1867): 605–616.

36. *Chappelle's Show*, season 2, episode 11, "Mandela Boot Camp & The Time Haters," dir. by Rusty Cundieff, aired March 31, 2004, on Comedy Central.

37. Glenda R. Carpio, *Laughing Fit to Kill: Black Humor in the Fictions of Slavery* (Oxford: Oxford University Press, 2008), 114.

38. *Chappelle's Show*, season 2, episode 11.

39. Psyche Williams-Forson, *Building Houses Out of Chicken Legs: Black Women, Food, and Power* (Chapel Hill: University of North Carolina Press, 2006), 38.

40. Williams-Forson, *Building Houses Out of Chicken Legs*, 49.

41. Dave Chappelle, *Killin' Them Softly*, dir. Stan Lathan, aired July 26, 2000, on Home Box Office.

42. Christopher Farley, "Dave Speaks," *Time*, May 14, 2005, 68.

43. Kevin Powell, "Heaven Hell Dave Chappelle: The Agonizing Return of the Funniest Man in America," *Esquire*, May 29, 2006, 147–148.

44. Robert Patterson, *The Psychic Hold of Slavery* (New Brunswick, NJ: Rutgers University Press 2016).

45. *Chappelle's Show*, season 3, episode 2.

46. *Chappelle's Show*, season 3, episode 2.

47. *Inside the Actor's Studio*, season 12, episode 11, "Dave Chappelle," aired February 12, 2006, on Ovation.

48. Powell, "Heaven Hell Dave Chappelle," 148.

49. *Chappelle's Show*, season 1, episode 1, "Popcopy & Clayton Bigsby," dir. Andre Allen, Rusty Cundieff, and Bobcat Goldthwait, aired January 22, 2003, on Comedy Central.

50. Farley, "Dave Speaks," 72.

51. Farley, "Dave Speaks," 70.

52. *The Oprah Winfrey Show*, season 22, episode 68, "His First TV Interview: Why Dave Chappelle Walked Away from $50 Million," aired February 3, 2006, Harpo Productions.

53. *Iconoclasts*, series 2, episode 6.

54. Houston Baker, *Blues, Ideology, and Afro-American Literature: A Vernacular Theory* (Chicago: University of Chicago Press, 1987).

55. Farley, "Dave Speaks," 73.

56. Carpio, *Laughing Fit to Kill*, 111.

57. Jason Zinoman, "A Somewhat Less Rebellious Rebel," *New York Times*, June 19, 2014.

58. Bambi Haggins, *Laughing Mad: The Black Comic Persona in Post-Soul America* (New Brunswick, NJ: Rutgers University Press, 2007), 178.

59. *Sticks and Stones*, dir. Stan Lathan, aired August 26, 2019, on Netflix.

60. *My Next Guest Needs No Introduction*, season 3, episode 3, "Dave Chappelle," dir. Helen M. Cho, aired on October 21, 2020 on Netflix. https://www.netflix.com/nz/title/80209096.

61. Netflix Is a Joke, "8:46—Dave Chappelle," YouTube video, 27:20, June 12, 2020, https://www.youtube.com/watch?v=3tR6mKcBbT4.

62. Netflix Is a Joke, "8:46—Dave Chappelle."

63. #SayHerName was in circulation before Breonna Taylor's death. It first became popular as a response to Sandra Bland's murder in 2015. The hashtag campaign builds on Kimberlé Crenshaw's theory of intersectionality to think through the ways that Black women are both vulnerable and erased from conversations of police brutality and state-sanctioned, extrajudicial violence. In other words, #SayHerName is invested in intervening in that patriarchy informs the way the Black Lives Matter movement prioritizes and privileges Black men's and boy's lives, loss, and potential. See Kimberlé Crenshaw, "Mapping the Margins: Intersectionality, Identity Politics, and Violence against Women of Color," *Stanford Law Review* 43, no. 6 (1991): 1241–1299; Kimberlé Crenshaw, Andrea J. Ritchie, Rachel Anspach, Rachel Gilmer, and Luke Harris, *Say Her Name: Resisting Police Brutality Against Black Women* (African American Policy Forum, Center for Intersectionality and Social Policy Studies, ebook, January 2016).

64. Danielle Morgan, *Laughing to Keep from Dying: African American Satire in the Twenty-First Century* (Urbana: University of Illinois Press, 2020), 93.

CHAPTER 3   INTEGRATIONIST INTIMACIES

1. Kevin Quashie, *The Sovereignty of Quiet: Beyond Resistance in Black Culture* (New Brunswick, NJ: Rutgers University Press, 2012), 76.

2. I use "postracial" here as I've written before as the attempt "to look beyond race or, more aptly, in spite of race to a homogenous future free from the wounds of racism." See my "Adam Mansbach's Postracial Imaginary in *Angry Black White Boy*," in *Neo-Passing: Performing Identity after Jim Crow*, ed. Mollie Godfrey and Vershawn Ashanti Young (Champaign: University of Illinois Press, 2018), 84–95.

3. Michel Foucault, *The History of Sexuality*, vol. 1, *An Introduction*, trans. Robert Hurley (New York: Vintage, 1990), 83.

4. Michael Kimmel, *Manhood in America: A Cultural History*, 3rd ed. (Oxford: Oxford University Press, 2012), 71.

5. Trudier Harris, *Exorcising Blackness: Historical and Literary Lynching and Burning Rituals* (Bloomington: Indiana University Press, 1984), 5.

6. Koritha Mitchell, *Living with Lynching: African American Lynching Plays, Performance, and Citizenship, 1890–1930* (Urbana: University of Illinois Press, 2012).

7. Sandy Alexandre, *The Properties of Violence* (Oxford: University Press of Mississippi, 2012), 4.

8. Foucault, *History of Sexuality*, 1:92.

9. Patricia Hill Collins, *Black Sexual Politics: African Americans, Gender, and the New Racism* (New York: Routledge, 2005), 56–57.

10. Audre Lorde, *Sister Outsider: Essays and Speeches* (Berkeley: Ten Speed Press, 2013), 53.

11. Hazel Carby, *Race Man* (Cambridge, MA: Harvard University Press, 1998), 21.

12. "Haysbert Thinks His '24' Role Helped Obama," *Today*, July 2, 2008, https://www.today.com/popculture/haysbert-thinks-his-24 -role-helped-obama-1C9413332.

13. Mia Mask and Ian Strachan, eds., *Poitier Revisited: Reconsidering a Black Icon in the Age of Obama* (New York: Bloomsbury Publishing, 2014), 2.

14. The Key of Awesome, "Crush on Obama," YouTube video, 3:19, June 13, 2007, https://www.youtube.com/watch?v =wKsoXHYICqU.

15. Elahe Izadi, "How Attractive Is Barack Obama? That Depends on Your Party Affiliation," *Washington Post*, October 15, 2014, https:// www.washingtonpost.com/news/the-fix/wp/2014/10/15/beauty -is-in-the-eye-of-the-partisan/.

16. Nathan Siegel, "Why You Find President Obama Attractive," *HuffPost*, November 15, 2014, https://www.ozy.com/news-and -politics/why-you-find-president-obama-attractive/37113/.

17. Throughout this book, I've used respectability politics as an enunciation of a Black heteronormative, middle-class value system that both resonates with White America as acceptable expressions of blackness. Black respectability politics creates for Black communities a kind of best practices for Black existence in predominantly White spaces; at worst it is a survival tactic of self-policing and victim blaming for expressions and articulations of blackness outside of the fluid concept of "respectable."

18. *In the Heat of the Night*, dir. Norman Jewison (The Mirisch Corporation, 1967); *The Defiant Ones*, dir. Stanley Kramer (Lomitas Productions and Curtleigh Productions, 1958).

19. Sharon Holland, *The Erotic Life of Racism* (Durham, NC: Duke University Press, 2012).

20. *Blackboard Jungle*, dir. Richard Brooks (Metro-Goldwyn-Mayer, 1955); *Lilies of the Field*, dir. Ralph Nelson (Rainbow Productions, 1963); *To Sir with Love*, dir. James Clavell (Columbia Pictures, 1967); and *Guess Who's Coming to Dinner*, dir. Stanley Kramer (Columbia Pictures, 1967).

21. Nicole Fleetwood, *Troubling Vision: Performance, Visuality, and Blackness* (Chicago: University of Chicago Press, 2011), 33.
22. Movieclips Classic Trailers, "Lilies of the Field Official Trailer #1–Sidney Poitier Movie (1963) HD," YouTube video, 3:13, October 6, 2012, https://www.youtube.com/watch?v=8aL0ml00S9Q.
23. Sharon Willis, *The Poitier Effect: Racial Melodrama and Fantasies of Reconciliation* (Minneapolis: University of Minnesota Press, 2015), 5.
24. Clifford Mason, "Why Does White America Love Poitier So?," *New York Times*, September 10, 1967, 23, 142.
25. Mason, "Why Does White America Love Poitier So?," 142.
26. Mason, "Why Does White America Love Poitier So?," 142.
27. Willis, *Poitier Effect*, 5.
28. *To Sir, with Love*, dir. James Clavell (Columbia Pictures, 1967).
29. Hortense Spillers, "Mama's Baby, Papa's Maybe: An American Grammar Book," *Diacritics* 17, no. 2 (Summer 1987): 80.
30. Saidiya Hartman, *Scenes of Subjection: Terror, Slavery, and Self-Making in Nineteenth-Century America* (New York: Oxford University Press, 1997), 85.
31. "I suggest that rape and the threat of rape influenced the development of a culture of dissemblance among Black women. By dissemblance I mean the behavior and attitudes of Black women that created the appearance of openness and disclosure but actually shielded the truth of their inner lives and selves from their oppressors." Darlene Clark Hine, "Rape and the Inner Lives of Black Women in the Middle West," *Signs* 14, no. 4 (1989): 912.
32. Chana Kai Lee, *For Freedom's Sake: The Life of Fannie Lou Hammer* (Urbana: University of Illinois, 1999), 9–10.
33. Aliyyah I. Abdur-Rahman, "'The Strangest Freaks of Despotism': Queer Sexuality in Antebellum African American Slave Narratives," *African American Review* 40, no. 2 (2006): 223.
34. Thomas A. Foster, "The Sexual Abuse of Black Men under American Slavery," *Journal of the History of Sexuality* 20, no. 3 (2011): 448.
35. Toni Morrison, *Beloved* (New York: Knopf Publishing, 1987); Frederick Douglass, *The Narrative of the Life of Frederick Douglass* (Boston: Anti-Slavery Office, 1845).
36. Danielle L. McGuire, *At the Dark End of the Street: Black Women, Rape, and Resistance—A New History of the Civil Rights Movement from Rosa Parks to the Rise of Black Power* (New York: Alfred A. Knopf Press, 2010), 167.
37. John Dittmer, *Local People: The Struggle for Civil Rights in Mississippi* (Urbana: University of Illinois Press, 1995), 263.
38. James Baldwin, *Going to Meet the Man* (New York: Dial Press, 1965).
39. The frequent references to Sidney Poitier in the novel and the possibility that he may be Not Sidney's father also evokes the real-life

story of David Hampton, the American conman and thief who was able to defraud a group of New Yorkers by presenting himself as Sidney Poitier's son. Hampton's story was later turned into the play *Six Degrees of Separation* (1990) by John Guare, which was the basis of the 1993 film of the same name directed by Fred Schepisi.

40. See *I Am Not Your Negro*, dir. Raoul Peck (Velvet Film, 2016).
41. Percival Everett, *I Am Not Sidney Poitier: A Novel* (Saint Paul: Graywolf Press, 2009).
42. Everett, *I Am Not Sidney Poitier*, 31.
43. In Paul Beatty's novel *The White Boy Shuffle* (New York: Houghton Mifflin, 1996), protagonist Gunnar Kaufman is sexually assaulted by his father and the assault is similarly described in an impressionistic way—through a description of what the color Black means to the protagonist. It is important to note that Kaufman is victimized later in the novel by two neighborhood girls, Betty and Veronica, and that the narration departs from the earlier abstract and solemn representation at the point.
44. Everett, *I Am Not Sidney Poitier*, 31–32.
45. Gayl Jones, *Corregidora* (Boston: Beacon Press, 1975), 184.
46. Jones, *Corregidora*, 184.
47. Ashraf H. A. Rushdy, "'Relate Sexual to Historical': Race, Resistance, and Desire in Gayl Jones's *Corregidora*," *African American Review* 34, no. 2 (2000): 280.
48. Jones, *Corregidora*, 67.
49. Everett, *I Am Not Sidney Poitier*, 35.
50. Everett, *I Am Not Sidney Poitier*, 37.
51. Vincent Woodard, *The Delectable Negro: Human Consumption and Homoeroticism with U.S. Slave Culture* (New York: New York University Press, 2014), 143.
52. *In the Heat of the Night*, dir. Norman Jewison (Walter Mirisch Corporation, 1967).
53. Everett, *I Am Not Sidney Poitier*, 36.
54. Everett, *I Am Not Sidney Poitier*, 50.
55. Everett, *I Am Not Sidney Poitier*, 50–51.
56. Rebecca Wanzo, *The Suffering Will Not Be Televised: African American Women and Sentimental Political Storytelling* (Albany: State University of New York Press, 2009), 120.
57. Everett, *I Am Not Sidney Poitier*, 58.

CHAPTER 4   THE PRESIDENT AND HIS TRANSLATOR

Epigraph: Audre Lorde, "The Uses of Anger," *Women's Studies Quarterly* 25, nos. 1–2 (Spring–Summer 1997): 280.

1. bell hooks, *We Real Cool: Black Men and Masculinity* (New York: Routledge, 2004), 97.

2. Miles White, *From Jim Crow to Jay-Z: Race, Rap, and the Performance of Masculinity* (Urbana: University of Illinois Press, 2011), 25.
3. Michael Kimmel, *Angry White Men: American Masculinity at the End of an Era* (New York: Nation, 2013).
4. William H. Grier and Price M. Cobbs, *Black Rage* (New York: Basic, 1968), 59.
5. Frantz Fanon, *Black Skin, White Masks* (New York: Grove Press, 1967), 50.
6. Brittney Cooper, *Eloquent Rage: A Black Feminist Discovers Her Superpower* (New York: St. Martin's Press, 2018), 1–2.
7. Kimmel, *Angry White Men*, 36.
8. Carol Anderson, "Ferguson Isn't about Black Rage against Cops. It's White Rage against Progress," *Washington Post*, August 29, 2014.
9. hooks, *We Real Cool*, 22.
10. Freddy Gray, "The Professorial President: Is Obama Actually Super-Smart, or Just Academic?," *Spectator*, October 6, 2012, https://www.spectator.co.uk/article/the-professorial-president-.
11. Hortense Spillers, "Destiny's Child: Obama and Election '08," *Boundary* 2, vol. 39 (2012), 9.
12. Sarah Ahmed, *The Cultural Politics of Emotions* (New York: Routledge, 2004) 184.
13. Barack Obama, "A More Perfect Union," March 18, 2008, National Constitution Center, https://constitutioncenter.org /amoreperfectunion/.
14. Obama, "A More Perfect Union."
15. Obama's campaign heavily featured Shepard Fairey's poster of Obama in blue and red with the word "HOPE."
16. "Obama's Fifth News Conference," *New York Times*, July 22, 2009, https://www.nytimes.com/2009/07/22/us/politics/22obama .transcript.html.
17. "Obama's Fifth News Conference."
18. President Obama Explains to att Lauer that BP Ass-kicking's on the way, YouTube, https://www.youtube.com/watch?v=KAdh QoIIhDk, accessed March 2019.
19. Richard Majors and Janet Billson, *Cool Pose: The Dilemmas of Black Manhood in America* (New York: Touchstone, 1992), 4.
20. Slow Jam the News with Barack Obama (Late Night With Jimmy Fallon, https://www.youtube.com/watch?v=vAFQIciWsF4, accessed July 2021.
21. Barack Obama, "President Obama complete remarks at 2015 White House Correspondents' Dinner (C-SPAN),"YouTube, https://www .youtube.com/watch?v=NM6d06ALBVA, accessed April 2019, 14:25–14:35.
22. White House Correspondents' Association, whca.net/history.htm, accessed August 2021.

23. From the late twentieth century to the end of Obama's presidency, the featured comedians are either late night television hosts that routinely offer edgy critiques of the political figures and the media or mock news shows on Comedy Central like *The Daily Show.*

24. Bambi Haggins, *Laughing Mad: The Black Comic Persona in Post-Soul America* (New Brunswick, NJ: Rutgers University Press, 2007), 25.

25. Wanda Sykes, Wanda Sykes at the 2009 White House Correspondents' Dinner, YouTube, https://www.youtube.com/watch?v=zmyRog2w4DI, accessed June 2020, 2:16–2:19.

26. Larry Wilmore, Larry Wilmore Complete remarks at 2016 White House Correspondence Association Dinner (CSPAN), YouTube, https://www.youtube.com/watch?v=1IDFt3BL7FA, accessed June 2020, 22:02–22:07.

27. Oxford English Dictionary, OED, https://www.oed.com/view/Entry/123402?redirectedFrom=mulatto, accessed June 2019.

28. Nella Larsen, *Quicksand* (New York: Knopf, 1928); Nella Larsen, *Passing* (New York, Knopf, 1929); and John M. Stahl, *Imitation of Life,* Universal Pictures, film (1934).

29. Larry Wilmore, https://www.youtube.com/watch?v=1IDFt3BL7FA, accessed June 2020, 22:02–22:07.

30. *Key and Peele*, season 4, episode 1 (2014).

31. Barack Obama, C-SPAN: President Obama at the 2011 White House Correspondents' Dinner, YouTube, https://www.youtube.com/watch?v=n9mzJhvC-8E, accessed June 2019, 2:50–3:35.

32. Barack Obama, President Obama at 2013 White House Correspondents' Dinner (C-SPAN), YouTube, https://www.youtube.com/watch?v=ON2XWvyePH8, accessed June 2019, 15:40–18:01.

33. *Key and Peele*, season 1, episode 1, "Bitch," dir. Peter Atencio, aired January 31, 2012, on Comedy Central.

34. *Key and Peele*, season 1, episode 1, 2012.

35. *Key and Peele*, season 1, episode 1, 2012.

36. *Key and Peele*, season 1, episode 1, 2012.

37. *Coach Carter*, dir. Thomas Charter, MTV films, film (2005); *Lean On Me*, dir. John G. Avildsen, Norman Twain Productions and Warner Bros., film (1989).

38. Elizabeth Blair, "For 'Black Nerds Everywhere,' Two Comedy Heroes," *NPR*, January 27, 2012, https://www.npr.org/2012/01/27/145838407/for-black-nerds-everywhere-two-comedy-heroes.

39. Blair, "For 'Black Nerds Everywhere.'"

40. Cooper, *Eloquent Rage*, 151.

41. David R. Williams, "Stress and the Mental Health of Populations of Color: Advancing Our Understanding of Race-Related Stressors," *Journal of Health and Social Behavior* 59, no. 4 (2018): 466–485.

CONCLUSION

1. Sherley Anne Williams, "Some Implications of a Womanist Theory," *Callaloo* 9, no. 2 (Spring 1986): 307.
2. LaMonda Horton-Stallings, "'Punked for Life': Paul Beatty's *The White Boy Shuffle* and Radical Black Masculinities," *African American Review* 43, no. 1 (Spring 2009): 103.
3. Williams, "Some Implications," 307.
4. John O. Killens, *The Cotillion, or, One Good Bull Is Half the Herd* (New York: Trident Press, 1971).
5. Bill Cosby, "Dr. Bill Cosby Speaks at the 50th Anniversary Commemoration of the *Brown v. Topeka Board of Education* Supreme Court Decision," *The Black Scholar* 34, no. 4 (May 22, 2004): 2–3.
6. "Unemployment in Black and White," *New York Times*, August 8, 2017, https://www.nytimes.com/2017/08/28/opinion /unemployment-in-black-and-white.html?searchResultPosition=1.
7. Jerrod Carmichael, *Home Videos*, HBO, film (2019); and *Sermon on the Mount*, HBO, film (2019)
8. *The Carmichael Show*, Morningside Entertainment and Universal Television (2015–2017); *Love at the Store*, HBO, film (2014) and *8*, HBO, film (2017).
9. Issa Rae, *Insecure*, HBO (2016–).
10. Issa Rae, *The Mis-Adventures of Awkward Black Girl*, YouTube, *The Mis-Adventures of Awkward Black Girl* (2011–2013).
11. Radha Blank, Hotep Hoteppin, Vimeo, 2016, https://vimeo.com /166421073.
12. Phoebe Robinson and Jessica Williams, *2 Dope Queens*, HBO (2016–2018); Robin Thede, *The Black Lady Sketch Show*, HBO (2019–).

Selected Bibliography

Abdur-Rahman, Aliyyah I. "'The Strangest Freaks of Despotism': Queer Sexuality in Antebellum African American Slave Narratives." *African American Review* 40, no. 2 (2006): 223–237.

Baker, Houston. *Blues, Ideology, and Afro-American Literature: A Vernacular Theory* (Chicago: University of Chicago Press, 1987).

Berlant, Lauren. *Cruel Optimism* (Durham, NC: Duke University Press, 2011).

Billig, Michael. *Laughter and Ridicule: Towards a Social Critique of Humour* (London: SAGE, 2005).

Brooks, Daphne. *Bodies in Dissent: Spectacular Performances of Race and Freedom, 1850–1910* (Durham, NC: Duke University Press, 2006).

Carby, Hazel Z. *Race Men* (Cambridge, MA: Harvard University Press, 1998).

Carpio, Glenda R. *Laughing Fit to Kill: Black Humor in the Fictions of Slavery* (Oxford: Oxford University Press, 2008).

Cooper, Brittney. *Beyond Respectability: The Intellectual Thought of Race Women* (Urbana: University of Illinois Press, 2017).

———. *Eloquent Rage: A Black Feminist Discovers Her Superpower* (New York: St. Martin's Press, 2018).

Cross Jr., William. "The Negro-to-Black Conversion Experience." *Black World* 20, no. 9 (1971): 13–27.

Dickson-Carr, Darryl. *African American Satire: The Sacredly Profane Novel* (Columbia: University of Missouri Press, 2001).

———. *Spoofing the Modern: Satire in the Harlem Renaissance* (Columbia: University of South Carolina Press, 2015).

Dittmer, John. *Local People: The Struggle for Civil Rights in Mississippi* (Urbana: University of Illinois Press, 1995).

Du Bois, W.E.B. "Criteria of Negro Art." *Crisis* 32 (October 1926): 290–297.

———. *The Souls of Black Folk: A Norton Critical Edition*, edited by Henry Louis Gates Jr. and Terri Hume Oliver (New York: W. W. Norton, 1999).

Dunbar, Paul Laurence. *The Collected Poetry of Paul Laurence Dunbar*, edited by Joanne M. Braxton (Charlottesville: University of Virginia Press, 1993).

Edwards, Erica. *Charisma and the Fictions of Black Leadership* (Minneapolis: University of Minnesota Press, 2012).

Ellison, Ralph. "Change the Joke and Slip the Yoke." *Partisan Review* 25, no. 2 (1958): 212–222.

Fanon, Frantz. *Black Skin, White Masks* (New York: Grove Press, 1967).

Fauset, Jessie. "The Gift of Laughter." In *The New Negro*, edited by Alain Locke, 161–167. (New York: Boni, 1925).

Fleetwood, Nicole. *Troubling Vision: Performance, Visuality, and Blackness* (Chicago: University of Chicago Press, 2011).

Foster, Thomas A. "The Sexual Abuse of Black Men under American Slavery." *Journal of the History of Sexuality* 20, no. 3 (2011): 445–464.

Freud, Sigmund. *Jokes and Their Relation to the Unconscious* (New York: W. W. Norton, 1960).

Frye, Northrop. *Anatomy of Criticism: Four Essays* (Princeton, NJ: Princeton University Press, 1957).

George, Nelson. *Hip Hop America* (New York: Penguin, 1998).

Gilroy, Paul. *The Black Atlantic: Modernity and Double-Consciousness* (Cambridge, MA: Harvard University Press, 1993).

Green, Viveca S. "'Deplorable' Satire: Alt-Right Memes, White Genocide Tweets, and Redpilling Normies." *Studies in American Humor* 5, no. 1 (2019): 31–69.

Grier, William H., and Price M. Cobbs. *Black Rage* (New York: Basic, 1968).

Haggins, Bambi. "In the Wake of 'The Nigger Pixie.'" In *Satire TV: Politics and Comedy in the Post-Network Era*, edited by Jonathan Gray and Jeffrey Jones, 233–251. (New York: New York University Press, 2009).

———. *Laughing Mad: The Black Comic Persona in Post-Soul America* (New Brunswick, NJ: Rutgers University Press, 2007).

Halberstam, Judith. *The Queer Art of Failure* (Durham, NC: Duke University Press, 2011).

Hartman, Saidiya. *Scenes of Subjection: Terror, Slavery, and Self-Making in Nineteenth-Century America* (Oxford: Oxford University Press, 1997).

Hine, Darlene Clark. "Rape and the Inner Lives of Black Women in the Middle West." *Signs* 14, no. 4 (1989): 912–920.

hooks, bell. *We Real Cool: Black Men and Masculinity* (New York: Routledge, 2004).

Hurston, Zora Neale. "Characteristics of Negro Expression." In *Within the Circle: An Anthology of African American Literary Criticism from the Harlem Renaissance to the Present*, edited by Angelyn Mitchell, 79–94. (Durham, NC: Duke University Press, 1994).

Iton, Richard. *In Search of the Black Fantastic: Politics and Popular Culture in the Post–Civil Rights Era* (New York: Oxford University Press, 2008).

Kimmel, Michael. *Angry White Men: American Masculinity at the End of an Era* (New York: Nation, 2013).

———. *Manhood in America: A Cultural History* (Oxford: Oxford University Press, 2012).

Knight, Charles A. *The Literature of Satire* (Cambridge: University of Cambridge Press, 2004).

Krefting, Rebecca. *All Joking Aside: American Humor and Its Discontents* (Baltimore: Johns Hopkins University Press, 2014).

Lee, Chana Kai. *For Freedom's Sake: The Life of Fannie Lou Hammer* (Urbana: University of Illinois, 1999).

Lorde, Audre. "The Uses of Anger." *Women's Studies Quarterly* 25, nos. 1–2 (Spring–Summer 1997): 278–285.

Lott, Eric. *Love and Theft: Blackface Minstrelsy and the American Working Class* (Oxford: Oxford University Press, 1993).

Manring, Maurice. *Slave in a Box: The Strange Career of Aunt Jemima* (Charlottesville: University of Virginia Press, 1998).

Mask, Mia, and Ian Strachan, eds. *Poitier Revisited: Reconsidering a Black Icon in the Age of Obama* (New York: Bloomsbury, 2014).

McGuire, Danielle L. *At the Dark End of the Street: Black Women, Rape, and Resistance—A New History of the Civil Rights Movement from Rosa Parks to the Rise of Black Power* (New York: Alfred A. Knopf Press, 2010).

Mizejewski, Linda. *Pretty/Funny: Women Comedians and Body Politics* (Austin: University of Texas Press, 2015).

Morrison, Toni. *Playing in the Dark: Whiteness and the Literary Imagination* (Cambridge, MA: Harvard University Press, 1992).

Moten, Fred. *In The Break: The Aesthetics of the Black Radical Tradition* (Minneapolis: University of Minnesota Press, 2003).

Munoz, Jose. *Disidentifications: Queers of Color and the Performance of Politics* (Minneapolis: University of Minnesota Press, 2013).

Neal, Mark Anthony. *Post-Soul Babies: Black Popular Culture and the Post-Soul Aesthetic* (New York: Routledge, 2002).

Nevin, Robert. "Stephen C. Foster and Negro Minstrelsy." *Atlantic* 20, no. 121 (November 1867): 608–616.

Nietzsche, Friedrich. *The Will to Power* (New York: Vintage, 1968).

Patterson, Orlando. *Slavery and Social Death: A Comparative Study* (Cambridge, MA: Harvard University Press, 1982).

Patterson, Robert. *Exodus Politics: Civil Rights and Leadership in African American Literature and Culture* (Charlottesville: University of Virginia Press, 2013).

Quashie, Kevin. *The Sovereignty of Quiet: Beyond Resistance in Black Culture* (New Brunswick, NJ: Rutgers University Press, 2012).

Rogin, Michael. *Blackface, White Noise: Jewish Immigrants in the Hollywood Melting Pot* (Berkeley: University of California Press, 1998).

Rushdy, Ashraf H. A. "'Relate Sexual to Historical': Race, Resistance, and Desire in Gayl Jones's *Corregidora*." *African American Review* 34, no. 2 (2000): 273–297.

Sharpe, Christina. *Monstrous Intimacies: Making Post-Slavery Subjects* (Durham, NC: Duke University Press, 2010).

Spillers, Hortense. "Mama's Baby, Papa's Maybe: An American Grammar Book." *Diacritics* 17, no. 2 (Summer 1987): 64–81.

Walcott, Rinaldo. "Reconstructing Manhood; or, the Drag of Black Masculinity." *Small Axe* 13, no. 1 (March 2009): 75–89.

Wanzo, Rebecca. *The Suffering Will Not Be Televised: African American Women and Sentimental Political Storytelling* (Albany: State University of New York Press, 2009).

Warren, Calvin. "Black Nihilism and the Politics of Hope." *New Centennial Review* 15, no. 1 (2015): 215–248.

Watkins, Mel. *African American Humor: The Best Black Comedy from Slavery to Today* (Chicago: Chicago Review Press, 2002).

West, Cornel. *Race Matters* (New York: Vintage, 1994).

White, Miles. *From Jim Crow to Jay-Z: Race, Rap, and the Performance of Masculinity* (Urbana: University of Illinois Press, 2011).

Williams, Sherley Ann. "Some Implications of a Womanist Theory." *Callaloo* 9, no. 2 (Spring 1986): 303–308.

Williams-Forson, Psyche. *Building Houses Out of Chicken Legs: Black Women, Food, and Power* (Chapel Hill: University of North Carolina Press, 2006).

Willis, Sharon. *The Poitier Effect: Racial Melodrama and Fantasies of Reconciliation* (Minneapolis: University of Minnesota Press, 2015).

Woodard, Vincent. *The Delectable Negro: Human Consumption and Homoeroticism with U.S. Slave Culture* (New York: New York University Press, 2014).

INDEX

Note: Illustrations are indicated by page numbers in *italics*.

Du Bois, W.E.B., 28, 32–38,
 42–43, 65, 92

Edwards, Erika, 35–36
Ellis, Trey, 13, 15
Ellison, Ralph, 10–11, 47, 66–67, 77
emasculation, 19–20, 107, 115
Erasure (Everett), 13, 15–16, 103–104
Ettinger, Amber Lee, 94
Everett, Percival, 13, 15–16, 24,
 28–29, 47, 59, 88–89, 93,
 102–112, 164n39

Fallon, Jimmy, 124
Fanon, Frantz, 116
feminism, Black, 14–15, 19–20,
 22, 25, 32
feminist theory, 5–6
Ferguson, Roderick, 25
Fleetwood, Nicole, 43, 95–96
Flight to Canada (Reed), 12, 57
Floyd, George, 84–85
Foster, Thomas A., 101
Foucault, Michel, 89, 91
Freud, Sigmund, 66
Frye, Northrop, 7
"fuckboy," 148

Gambetti, Zeynep, 21
gangsta rap, 63
Garza, Alicia, 122
Gates, Henry Louis, 121–122
gender: American Dream and,
 31–32; anger and, 116; Beatty
 and, 50; Du Bois and, 36; in
 Insecure, 147–148; nihilism and,
 33, 35. *See also* masculinity,
 Black; patriarchy; women
George, Nelson, 64

*George Washington Carver Crossing
 the Delaware: Page from an
 American History Textbook*
 (Colescott), 13
Gilroy, Paul, 38
gradualism, 97
Greenlee, Sam, 12, 57
Grier, William, 115–116
Griffin, Dustin, 9–10
Griffith, D. W., 64–65, 90
Guerrero, Lisa, 57

Haggins, Bambi, 61–62
Half Baked (film), 61
Hamer, Fanny Lou, 100–101
Harlem Renaissance, 10, 12
Harris, Trudier, 90
Hartman, Saidiya, 100
Heidegger, Martin, 40
Henson, Josiah, 12
Hine, Darlene Clark, 100, 164n31
hip-hop, 62–63
*History of Sexuality, The: An
 Introduction* (Foucault), 91
Hitchens, Christopher, 18
Holland, Sharon, 98
Hollywood Shuffle (film), 13
Home Videos (Carmichael), 146–147
hooks, bell, 114–115, 117
hope, 31, 39, 118–119
Horton-Stallings, LaMonda,
 110, 141
"Hotep Hoteppin" (Blank), 148
How to Rent a Negro (ayo), 13
humor: integrationist, 145; joy of,
 66–67; masculinity and, 143;
 meaning-making and, 6–7;
 oppression and, 6; racism and,
 6. *See also* satire

About the Author

Brandon J. Manning is an assistant professor of Black literature and culture in the Department of English and a core faculty member in the Department of Comparative Race and Ethnic Studies at Texas Christian University. He has published numerous essays and coedited a special issue of *The Black Scholar* on Black masculinities and the matter of vulnerability.